"Simon's book is a jewel—a resource that I constantly refer to and recommend to others. Everyone from career seekers to corporate leaders should own this gem!"

—Tina Thomson,
Former CEO of the Businesswomen's
Association of South Africa

"There are many 'motivators' in the marketplace. I believe, however, that Simon Bailey has a unique persona and critical insight into the human psyche that allows him to connect deeply with people who want to dream and envision something better for themselves. Simon brings aspirations into reach and does it with a compelling energy. Most importantly, he is a man who has walked the talk and, therefore, has a legitimacy that serves as the foundation of his concepts."

—John Bearden, President & CEO,
GMAC Home Services

"Thank you, Simon, for these gems and nuggets of brilliance. You have put your heart and soul into this masterwork. I was not only inspired, but also empowered by your impressive collection of thoughts, words and ideas. Your message of releasing brilliance is manifested in this timely and much needed book. Everyone can benefit from reading it and internalizing the lessons you have so generously shared with the world. Bravo! We all now have something worth reading."

—George C. Fraser, Author, *Success Runs In Our Race*

"The first time I met Simon Bailey, I knew I had met someone destined for an amazing journey. Even then, many years ago, there was an obvious 'brilliance' that exuded from Simon. So it's not surprising that out of the fabric of Simon's life has come this exhortation, *Release Your Brilliance*. It is written with all the passion of one who has truly thrived by accepting his Universal Assignment and sharing that knowledge with others."

—Rick Goings, Chairman & CEO,
Tupperware Brands Corporation

"Whether you're a CEO or aspiring to be one, you are the only one who can lead yourself to new ways of being, doing and having. Simon Bailey helps unlock the mystery of that process. Inner treasures await you. Release your brilliance and find them."

—Jane Toombs, Executive Director,
CEO Council of Tampa Bay (Florida)

Release Your Brilliance

Brilliance

The 4 Steps to Transforming
Your Life and Revealing Your
Genius to the World

SIMON T. BAILEY

HARPER
BUSINESS

An Imprint of HarperCollins*Publishers*
www.harpercollins.com

To my father: You are the best dad in the entire world. Thanks for teaching me how to be a real man. You are my hero, my role model, and my master teacher. I want Daniel's and Madison's children to be like you and Mom. I love you, Dad, because you are brilliant!

To my mother: You told me that I was special when I was still a tiny seed in your womb. As I approach forty years of being on this earth, I realize that you are the really special one. Thanks for being brilliant. I love you.

HarperCollins books may be purchased for educational, business, or sales promotional use. For information, please e-mail the Special Markets Department at SPsales@harpercollins.com.

Designed by Renato Stanisic

18 19 20 PC/LSC 20 19 18 17 16 15 14 13 12

Library of Congress Cataloging-in-Publication Data

Bailey, Simon T.
    Release your brilliance : the 4 steps to transforming your life and revealing your genius to the world / Simon T. Bailey. — [Rev. ed.].
        p. cm.
    ISBN 978-0-06-145187-4
    1. Self-actualization (Psychology)   I. Title.

BF637.S4B32 2007

158.1—dc22   2007019995

CONTENTS

A DIAMOND IN THE ROUGH

"EACH OF US IS LIKE A DIAMOND, AND EACH OF US HAS THE POTENTIAL TO BE BRILLIANT."

Y ou hold in your hands a book that can transform your life. How do I know? Because the concepts and ideas presented here altered my life forever. *Release Your Brilliance* is a complete transformational system. Just as a master cutter reshapes a rough stone, changing it into a brilliant diamond, you can use this system to reshape your life, open the vault deep inside you, and showcase your diamond-like brilliance to the world.

This book is for every diamond in the rough who wants to release his or her brilliance. If you . . .

. . . seek a deeper spiritual meaning to life;

. . . have hit the wall—professionally, personally, physically, or emotionally;

. . . sense that you have the potential to do something great with your life, but don't have a clue what that might be;

. . . desire to discover what you can offer the ever-changing global workplace;

. . . long for authentic relationships;

. . . believe the rest of your life will be the best of your life;

. . . recognize your divine assignment and are content, but want to contribute even more;

. . . feel unfulfilled in your career, working only for the paycheck and benefits;

. . . miss the fun and excitement of life;

. . . find that you are consistently discouraged;

. . . want to stretch and grow as a person;

then I invite you to embark on this transformation with me.

Have you ever wondered why some people seemingly get all the breaks, have all the good looks, find all the great opportunities, and achieve all the success they desire? They live their lives in such a way that people beat a path to their doorstep. I used to wonder about that a lot. Why them and not me?

Actually, I wondered about that for the first thirty-two years of my life as I struggled with disillusionment, defeat, desolation, and despair. I felt my life was a mistake. It seemed as if I were living in a wilderness, alone and disconnected from the mainstream of society. I tried to fit in and get people to like me, but I didn't even like myself. I had no self-esteem, self-confidence, or self-worth. I often wondered if I would be better off dead.

You see, I was living in a world where young black men were portrayed as addicts, criminals, dropouts, and deadbeat dads. Was this what I was to aspire to? The odds were against black males succeeding in America. I believed that my color was my curse. As a boy, another kid once told me that I was "black as tar and ugly as dirt." Those words penetrated my heart. Whoever said that words can never hurt you was flat-out clueless!

I believed that if my skin were white, my hair blond, and my eyes blue, I would be accepted. I resented my parents and wished I had been born into a white family. Everything that was portrayed in the media, everything I saw in my neighborhood and at my school, implied that white was right and black was wrong. I was living in the ghetto—not just a physical ghetto, but a mental ghetto. I believed it was impossible for me to succeed at anything. I was a young man struggling to find my place in the world and to make sense of it all. There were many nights I lay awake and stared at the ceiling, wondering, "How will my life turn out? What will I become?"

My life was transformed when I met life coach Dr. Mark Chironna. He said to me, "You've been stuck in your body and in your mind, acting like you've been cursed because of the color of your skin. You weren't born to fit in. *You were born to be brilliant.*" He saw through my pain and convinced me it was time to let my light shine. I knew in my soul that I was born for more, but I didn't know how to break free of the beliefs that held me down.

Dr. Chironna invited me to embrace the reality and the timeless truth that black—like all colors—really is beautiful. He knows this is true because, although Mark is a white man, he and his wife have adopted two

African-American boys. He encouraged me to find, define, and shape my core talents and skills. That day—which I'll never forget—I cried like a baby, pouring out my pain until I couldn't cry anymore.

I accepted his invitation and started an aggressive plan to reframe my world. I read books, kept a journal, actively participated in life-coaching sessions, and did the deep work of dealing with my pain. I realized that nothing was going to change in my life until *I* changed. I had to transform my thinking, my beliefs, and my actions and take responsibility for the core areas of my life. I cried, I laughed, I examined my life, and I worked—*hard*—for seven years straight.

The transformation has been nothing short of miraculous, even if I do say so myself. I brought order to my chaotic internal world and took control of my stinking thinking. I learned to forgive myself and not to wallow in the mud. I became filled with belief, confidence, and hope for the future. Today, I live my life by design instead of by accident. I live with brilliant expectancy—I expect to have incredible experiences every hour of every day. And I've been blessed to be able to connect with some of the most brilliant people on the planet. Truly, each day is a treasured gift.

During my seven-year transformation, I became curious about what Dr. Chironna had said—that I was born to be brilliant. I wanted to understand how I could be born brilliant and yet be so dull and tarnished by the age of thirty-two. One day, I found a clue in a book I was reading called *Acres of Diamonds* by Russell Conwell.

His simple message transformed my thinking, and I had an epiphany: *Each of us is like a diamond, and each of us has the potential to be brilliant.* I was intrigued, so I began to research diamonds. The more I discovered, the more I realized that a diamond is the perfect metaphor to understand how we can become all that we were meant to be.

A diamond begins as carbon in the molten magma deep inside the earth. It then undergoes an absolutely amazing Evolutionary Transformation, first to become "rough" stone, and ultimately, the exquisite gemstone we value so highly.

EVOLUTIONARY TRANSFORMATION

Evolution is a process of change from a lower, simpler state to a higher, more complex or improved state.

Transform means to change in form, nature, or function.

Just as a diamond is transformed from carbon to rough stone to dazzling gemstone, we, too, can undergo an Evolutionary Transformation. No other animal on the planet can transform itself and its circumstances like a human being can. No matter where you are in your life, no matter what has happened to you in the past, you have the potential to transform yourself into a brilliant diamond. Your geography and your biography do not determine your destiny. Regardless of your starting point, you *can* evolve to a higher and better state.

My research led me to even more questions: What is

brilliance? Why is it important? How does it make a difference in the world?

Simply put, *releasing your brilliance* means releasing the genius within you. It's living from the inside out—finding your inner light and letting it shine for the whole world to see. It's discovering and leveraging your unique talents and your pure, intuitive intelligence.

Of the many characteristics that contribute to a diamond's beauty, brilliance is the most important, bar none. Brilliance is the life of the diamond; it is the burst of white light, the flash and the sparkle that captures our attention. Everyone notices a brilliant diamond—it seems to explode with light, eliciting "oohs" and "aahs" from those nearby.

And so it is when you release *your* brilliance. You have a certain vibrant energy that attracts the attention of those around you. You have "it"—a special, distinctive quality that's difficult to describe. It's more than presence, charisma, or enthusiasm. It's something much bigger and deeper. Brilliance has nothing to do with impressing people, but everything to do with allowing your light to shine and illuminate someone else's darkness.

Why is releasing your brilliance important? Well, let's consider what happens when you *don't* release your brilliance. When you operate outside of your brilliance, you become disengaged from life. You work and live to meet your daily needs rather than to maximize your potential. You simply exist from day to day, without much passion or enthusiasm for life. Meanwhile, your talents remain untapped, buried somewhere deep inside. This is an awful way to live. And it drags down those you care about—your family and friends.

Life shouldn't be that way—and it doesn't have to be. When you release your brilliance, you feel alive, connected, and uplifted. You use your talents and gifts to breathe life into everything and everyone around you. Your family, friends, co-workers, and even your organization all benefit from your brilliance. Imagine what would happen if each person on Earth simply focused on releasing his or her brilliance. Truly, the planet would experience an Evolutionary Transformation unlike anything mankind has ever seen.

When I finally embraced and began to leverage my core gifts, talents, and abilities, the floodgates opened for me. I found my genius. I discovered how to release my brilliance, and I discovered that diamonds truly are forever.

Through my work, I've connected with literally tens of thousands of people—some in person, some through e-mail, and many through phone calls. It saddens me how often I hear from people who feel trapped. I've lost track of the hours I've spent listening to bright men and women share how frustrated they are with their lives. Many of them were vibrant and brilliant at one time, but somewhere along the way they lost their energy and luster.

These experiences got me thinking—if each of us has the potential to release the brilliance of our inner diamond, why don't more of us do it? Why do some people shine while others don't? The questions led to more research, as well as more introspection and dissection of my own life. Eventually, I found what I believe to be the answer: *Because we've forgotten how to shine. We've forgotten that we are, in fact, priceless diamonds with a brilliance all our own.*

Every child is born with brilliance. No one is overlooked. No one is untouched. The essence of brilliance is in all of us, including you. When we are young, the world cherishes and celebrates our genius, our special gifts and talents. But as we grow older, our brilliance loses its luster.

Howard Gardner, Professor of Education at Harvard, has studied intelligence for more than twenty years and has developed methods to test the multiple intelligences of humans from birth to adulthood. (For more on this research and the concept of multiple intelligences, read his book *Frames of Mind: The Theory of Multiple Intelligences.*) Through his research, Gardner and his colleagues found that virtually all of the children they tested were at the genius level through the age of four. However, by age twenty, only 10 percent of the same children were at the genius level, and over age twenty, the number dropped to 2 percent!

It makes you wonder: What happened to the children's genius? Where did it go?

Actually, it didn't go anywhere. It's still there, but it's hidden deep within them. People are born brilliant and then spend the rest of their lives having their brilliance buried by virtually everyone around them.

As children, just as we are ramping up to explore all the spectacular wonders of the big world around us, that world starts to impose its judgments on us. Our parents, even though they mean well, are the first to stifle our genius with their words: "Be good!" "Put it down!" "You can't do that!" "I don't care what you think, just do what I say!" When we go to school, our teachers and classmates join in: "Color inside the lines!" "Do it this way." "That's a dumb question." "You're not doing it right!"

Until they go to school, children are unbelievably curious. Ironically, school often discourages curiosity because it encourages conformity, and conformity robs us of our creativity. Sadly, to succeed in our traditional educational system, we must often ignore our genius. It's almost as if the more educated we become, the more our brilliance is diffused. Author R. S. Ingersoll once said, "Colleges are places where pebbles are polished and diamonds are dimmed."

Clearly, parents and teachers don't intend to harm us. In fact, it's quite the opposite—they want to protect and help us. And of course, for the most part, they do. And yet there are aspects of our upbringing that confine and restrict our brilliance. Gradually, we come to believe that we are capable of fewer and fewer things. Eventually, it's been so long since our brilliance shone that we can't remember what it felt like, and we forget that we ever had genius and special talents to begin with.

But the soul doesn't forget.

It knows the world needs your unique gifts. So it takes

your brilliance and locks it away in a vault deep within you for safekeeping until it can safely shine again.

As the years go by, others continue to teach you that your special genius isn't valuable—bosses, friends, spouses, sometimes even your own children! No one acknowledges your brilliance anymore, not even you.

Eventually, you forget the vault even exists.

So you settle for who you are, instead of striving for who you were meant to be. You become just another "zebra in the herd" and compare yourself to everyone else. John Mason, author of *An Enemy Called Average*, puts it this way: "People are born originals, but die copies."

If you're like most people, you probably experience brief moments when the vault opens and a glimmer of your brilliance is released. In these moments of inspiration, when you catch just a glimpse of your destiny, you feel fully alive—energized, connected, in the flow. And then the vault slams shut again. And because you don't know the combination, you can't reopen it. So you return to the comfort zone, settling for a lackluster existence. *The most frustrating feeling in the world is to touch what could be your brilliant future and then to feel it slip from your grasp.*

So here we are. Your brilliance is locked up in the vault buried deep inside of you, and you stopped looking for the combination years ago. There's been no one to help you find a way to unlock the vault and release your hidden brilliance. Until now. . . .

I wrote this book to give you the combination to your vault, to help you discover the precious gifts and talents within, and to guide you as you transform your life. My mission is to reawaken the genius inside of you and to rekindle the light that has been dimmed. I know from experience that you *can* unlock the vault. You can access the brilliance that lies hidden within you. But to do that requires evaluating your life, examining your beliefs, and acting on your insights. Only you can unlock the vault—it must be opened from the inside out.

Some people would like you to believe that success is rare. Perhaps these are the same people who started the myth that diamonds are rare. Don't fall for either story. In fact, natural diamonds are no more rare than many other gems. Likewise, success is not rare, and it's not a privilege reserved for special or lucky people. The truth is, *you* are a diamond, and you have the potential for brilliant success. You just have to learn how to release it.

I'm sure you've heard the expression *diamond in the rough*. According to *Merriam-Webster's Collegiate Dictionary*, it means "one having exceptional qualities or potential, but lacking refinement or polish." When diamonds are mined or found, they actually are very rough. Looking at them, you might never believe the dazzling beauty that lies within the stone. But after being cut and polished, the radiant gem is revealed. Similarly, the potential for greatness already exists within each of us. Heather Bonham, a science teacher in Buffalo, New York, eloquently expressed it this way in a recent article: "All of us are diamonds. Some of us are still in the intense process of being pressed together and purified by fire. Others are diamonds in the rough, waiting for the jeweler to polish off our rough edges, transforming our surfaces into brilliant, light-reflecting facets."

My friend, wherever you are in your journey toward brilliance, this book has something to help you polish your diamond and shine even more brilliantly. I invite you to transition into a renaissance season in which you open new doors of opportunity and create new realities. In this era of your life, you will

Reawaken to why you were born into this time.
Rekindle the fire of hope, life, love, happiness, and belief.
Recover every ounce of spiritual energy that has leaked out of you.
Renew your faith to walk through new doors of opportunity.
Reconnect to your unique gifts and create your future.

Too often in life we wait for someone to give us permission to do something. Today, I'm giving you the go-ahead. Simon Says . . . *Release Your Brilliance.*

A GEM FOR YOU
Your geography and your biography do not determine your destiny.

CUTTING THE DIAMOND

USING THIS BOOK TO RELEASE YOUR BRILLIANCE

> "I'M JUST AN OLD CHUNK OF COAL, BUT I'M GONNA BE A DIAMOND SOME DAY. I'M GONNA GROW AND GLOW 'TIL I'M SO PURE PERFECT, I'M GONNA PUT A SMILE ON EV'RYBODY'S FACE."
>
> —BILLY JOE SHAVER, FROM THE SONG "I'M JUST AN OLD CHUNK OF COAL"

Most of us know at least a little bit about diamonds: They're stunning, valuable, and highly treasured. But did you know that diamonds go through an amazing evolution to become the sparkling gems we treasure? Most diamonds we see today were formed millions (if not billions) of years ago when carbon was subjected to intense heat and pressure. Over eons, the carbon crystallized into diamond. Powerful magma eruptions then brought the diamond-bearing ore to within a mile of the earth's surface.

Even after a rough diamond is mined, it still must go through a lengthy and exacting process of refining, cutting, and polishing. The first stop for the rough stone is with the marker, who carefully examines it and marks where it should be cleaved. The stone then goes to either a sawyer or a cleaver, who both perform essentially the same task: cutting the diamond to bring out the profile that will determine its shape. Sawing is a lengthy process. Cleaving, done with a sharp blow of a hammer on a blade across the stone, takes only moments. Next, the rough diamond is worked on by highly skilled and specialized cutters: The blocker cuts the general shape of the diamond, and the brilliandeers then cut and polish the facets.

A facet is a flat surface that is cut into a diamond and then polished to increase the diamond's brilliance and beauty. The crown facets (on the top of the diamond) and the pavilion facets (on the bottom) are refined into even more facets, resulting in a fully polished diamond that can have an astounding number of facets. A radiant-cut diamond, for example, has a total of seventy facets.

Diamond brilliance is defined as the reflection of white light from the facets. Each facet is precisely placed and masterfully shaped to maximize the brilliance of the stone. The light bouncing between the facets creates *scintillation*—the flash and fire you see when you move a diamond in the light. The more polished the facets, the more light that can pass through them, and the more brilliantly the diamond will shine.

Your journey to releasing your brilliance is much like the journey a diamond takes from rough stone to polished gem. Like the marker, you must closely examine your life to decide where changes are needed so that you can begin to cut away the unnecessary, unproductive, and unhealthy aspects. On your journey, there will be "aha!" moments—moments of truth—when something will suddenly become crystal clear for the first time. In those magical moments, it will be as if a master cleaver is opening your consciousness with one artful blow, revealing the knowledge you've been seeking.

Reaching the point where you can live your brilliance day in and day out involves a four-step process. The four Cs, the factors that determine a diamond's quality, represent the steps you will take in your personal transformation. The first step is seeking **Clarity** or profound insight. Next is **Color**—discovering your pure beliefs and reclaiming your authentic self. Step three, **Cut**, is about taking bold action. The final step is **Carat**—deciding just how big a diamond you want to be.

In Part I of this book, you'll discover the source of your brilliance. In Part II, I will walk you step-by-step through the four Cs, the process of releasing your potential. Just as a diamond has many facets, you also have many facets—the distinct thoughts, beliefs, and actions that make up who you are. Consequently, each chapter represents a personal facet that must be polished in order to discover the gem that is *you*.

No doubt you'll recognize some familiar principles and concepts. Realize there is nothing new under the sun. If it's new, it's not true; and if it's true, it's not new. All truths, insights, and wisdom already exist in the universe, waiting for a voice to articulate their meaning and impact on your life.

As you discover each facet, the following tools will help you initiate your transformation to a brilliant diamond:

- **Personal Appraisal.** Just as a jewelry appraisal assesses the value of a piece of jewelry, the Personal Appraisal will help you identify and clarify your value and worth. Each question will get you thinking and encourage you to dig deeper into the mine of your diamond brilliance. Write down your response to each question, and then periodically review your answers so you can see and track your progress.
- **Diamond Polishing.** This tool involves three action steps—the keys to unlocking your potential. As with a diamond, the more you polish your facets, the more you will begin to release your brilliance from the inside out.
- **A Gem for You.** These quotes sum up the essence of each facet and encapsulate the meaning of the message. Teach this truth to others and your light will shine even brighter.

Scattered throughout the book you'll discover brief passages called "Living Diamonds." These stories illustrate how ordinary people have applied the concepts and principles in this book to unlock their hidden vaults and release their brilliance. The stories are from people that I've met through my work and through my newsletter, which reaches thousands of people around the world. I've changed their names so they can share their innermost thoughts with you and still maintain their privacy. I hope their experiences will inspire you as they did me.

To get the most benefit from *Release Your Brilliance*, read through the entire book once. Then determine the best way to implement the transformational system in your own life. Everyone's journey will be different. You may want to start from the beginning and work through the facets in the order in which they're presented. Or you may find that some facets are more significant in your life. Choose those principles to practice first, as they will meet your greatest needs. Act immediately on the one concept that ignites your inner drive and resonates with your innermost being. Then move on to the next facet.

Work at your own pace: You can complete one facet each week or one each month. This is thought-provoking stuff, so give the Personal Appraisal and Daily Polishing exercises the time they deserve. The whole point of this book is to get you to reflect on your life and deeply consider your future. That takes time. There's no prize for the person who finishes first. Remember how long it takes to create a diamond—and how magnificent the results are. The prize is the diamond you become and what you discover about yourself on the journey.

However you choose to implement the concepts, I strongly urge you to find an Accountability Partner who will also read the book, so the two of you can share what you're learning and what actions you will take. Diamond is the hardest substance on Earth. The only thing that can cut a diamond is another diamond. The partnership you forge with your Accountability Partner will enable you to nip at each other's heels and keep each other on track toward releasing your brilliance.

Think of your Accountability Partner as your personal Brilliandeer—the one who will help you cut and polish your facets. A Brilliandeer polishes a diamond by lowering it onto a spinning plate, carefully adjusting the pressure and exercising care not to damage the diamond. Your Accountability Partner will do the same for you. He or she will ask you the difficult questions, hold your feet to the fire, and exert just enough pressure to maximize the polish of your facets.

I suggest you choose someone who knows you fairly well and whose feedback you trust. Or, if you prefer, work with a few people in a small group. Many people find the dynamics that come from working through a process like this in a small group are particularly exciting and worthwhile. Whichever approach you choose—individual or small group—just be sure you set a regular time to work through these concepts together.

And finally, be sure to come and visit me at www. ReleasingBrilliance.com, where you can subscribe to my free e-zine and find exercises, tips, and tools to further help you release your brilliance. In fact, when you see the ♦ icon throughout the book, you'll know there are resources on my website for polishing that particular facet.

Release Your Brilliance was written for you. I hope there will be times when it will seem as if we know each other. Well, guess what? We do! I'm talking directly to you. It's my intention to walk beside you and give you a fresh outlook on why the world needs your brilliance—right now!

I invite you to allow this book to be your catalyst for brilliance. As you read it, study it, contemplate it, and digest the intent behind the content, you will begin an amazing journey. If you will immerse yourself in this journey, you'll discover the brilliance I'm certain is hidden within you.

A Gem for You
It takes a diamond to cut a diamond.

PART ONE

THE ESSENCE OF BRILLIANCE

"AT THE MOMENT A CHILD IS BORN, IT IS
ALREADY REALLY BRILLIANT. IT PICKS UP LANGUAGE,
MUCH BETTER THAN A DOCTOR OF PHILOSOPHY
IN ANY SUBJECT, IN ONLY TWO YEARS. AND IT IS
A MASTER OF IT BY THREE OR FOUR."

–TONY BUZAN, PEAK-PERFORMANCE EXPERT

When you were in the womb preparing to make your entrance into the world, family and friends anticipated your arrival and showered your mother with gifts of congratulations. After your birth, announcements and pictures were mailed. Long-distance calls were made from coast to coast, telling people the gift of *You* had finally arrived. Family and friends came from near and far to see, hold, and kiss this incredible gift of life.

Why all the hoopla about You? First of all, you were, and still are, a one-of-a-kind, priceless diamond of unlimited potential wrapped in flesh. No one else on Earth has your fingerprints, your smile, your signature—or your brilliance. Your uniqueness is your human signature. Hundreds, thousands, perhaps millions of people need your giftedness. You were born to release your brilliance and leave a mark on the universe. You are supposed to be here!

Everything you need to be brilliant is already inside you. Your source of brilliance is your genius—the one thing that you do better than anyone else. You have incredible gifts, and once you exercise these gifts, you'll evolve from merely existing to fully living. When you rediscover your brilliance and release it from the vault, you'll move along the Brilliance Continuum from dull to dazzling. You'll begin to realize why you're here on Earth and understand how to create your future from the inside out.

EXERCISE: *The Brilliance Continuum*

Below is a model to help you identify your current ability to release your brilliance. Dazzling, of course, is what you're striving for. Draw a vertical line to indicate where you believe you are right now on the Brilliance Continuum

DULL   **DAZZLING**

A good friend recently told me that he feels stuck professionally and personally, but that he doesn't know how to get out of his rut. He's read the books and attended the success seminars. He's watched others ascend the ladder of success. But when he's tried to do the same, it has seemed as if he couldn't reach the rungs. He has spent thousands of dollars on personal development, but he hasn't internalized it and applied it to his life. As he gets older—he's in his forties— he feels that he's running out of time.

Do you know anyone like that? People who are unhappy, unfulfilled, and unsettled, yet don't know what to do? They sit idly by, admiring everyone else, but have never done the work to find the essence of their own brilliance. Or if they have, they play it safe and talk themselves out of going after what's most alive in their hearts.

To me, people are like fine wines—they only get better with time. I truly believe it's never too late to find and release your brilliance. If Colonel Sanders could start Kentucky Fried Chicken in his sixties and Ronald Reagan could become President of the United States at sixty-nine, why should you feel limited by age?

Brilliance is inside each and every one of us! Brilliance is not just for pretty people or smart people or rich people. It is available to anyone and everyone who seeks it. That includes YOU!

Don't keep your brilliance hidden. Unlock the vault of your potential, and bring your genius out in the open for everyone to see!

A Gem for You
Everything you need to be brilliant is already inside you.

FACET: DISCOVER YOUR UNIVERSAL ASSIGNMENT

> "REALLY BELIEVE IN YOUR HEART OF HEARTS
> THAT YOUR FUNDAMENTAL PURPOSE, THE REASON FOR
> BEING, IS TO ENLARGE THE LIVES OF OTHERS. YOUR LIFE
> WILL BE ENLARGED ALSO. AND ALL OF THE OTHER
> THINGS WE HAVE BEEN TAUGHT TO CONCENTRATE ON
> WILL TAKE CARE OF THEMSELVES."
>
> —PETE THIGPEN, EXECUTIVE RESERVES

Nothing is here by accident. Everything on Earth has a divine assignment. Deep within the soul of each of us is a desire to know why we're here and how we can leave the world a better place. Perhaps you haven't yet reached that point. But eventually, you will ask the billion-dollar question: "Why am I here?"

The moment you pose the question, your heart and mind will begin to review your life story—what has been, what is, and what the future might be—and search for a scene that will complete that story. More than likely, when thinking about your life story up to this point, you think about *what* has happened—the events of your life. But the older you get, the more you begin to think about the *why* of life. As you mature, you begin to appreciate that life is more than a paycheck, a title, or a business card. You come to understand that who you are is so much more than what you do, where you live, and how much money you make.

So, why are you here? Even if you don't know the answer to that question, I do. Quite simply, you are here to complete your **Universal Assignment**. Yes, that's right, the universe has an assignment for you. And you are the only person on this planet of 6.5 billion people that can fulfill that assignment. You are here on Earth for a very specific reason. There is a void in the world that needs your touch, your insight, your wisdom, your magic. You are here to be different and to make a difference. You are here at this time in history to make a mark that only you can make. Your Universal Assignment is about how you shine and illuminate the lives of others.

Years ago, I was as lost as a goose in a blizzard! Professionally, I was working hard enough to keep a job, but just enough to keep from getting fired. I was going through the motions because, like most people, my bills were screaming louder than my dreams. My desires and wishes for blissful happiness and a purposeful life had vanished. Then I had one of those rare, defining moments that has a lasting impact on your life. The company I worked for had sent me to Paris on a consulting project with a 300-year-old European bank. During a presentation before one thousand of the bank's managers, I found my brilliance. I discovered "the me I had always wanted to be."

Since then, I've realized that my Universal Assignment is to inspire 10 percent of the 6.5 billion people on the planet to find their passion and release their brilliance.

How about you? Have you found the YOU you've always wanted to be?

The Greek philosopher Aristotle said, "Where your talents and the needs of the world cross, therein lies your vocation." I like to say, ". . . therein lies your Universal Assignment." You will find your Universal Assignment at the point where your talents, skills, abilities, and gifts intersect with a void or a need in the world around you. Think about what makes you original and special. What do you do better than anyone else? What do people tell you you're great at? Now, stop and listen to what keeps knocking on the door of your heart that you've been ignoring. Pay attention to the restlessness in your spirit and your soul. Any problem, issue, or situation that nags at you or aggravates you is a clue to your Universal Assignment. And finally, think about the point where those two aspects intersect—how can you use those special qualities that are uniquely yours to resolve the issue that is most important to you?

At this point, you might feel overwhelmed, thinking that your Universal Assignment has to be something profound, like feeding the homeless or curing cancer. *Your Universal Assignment is not necessarily to touch everyone; it's to touch someone.* Perhaps you'll have an impact on someone who then goes on to touch thousands of others. Perhaps you'll be the diamond that polishes another diamond and makes it shine more brilliantly. Even if you never grace the cover of a magazine or write a check to charity for a million dollars, you're still a person of purpose. Purpose is not some big thing you do "out there," it is a big thing you do "in here," inside yourself.

How do you know when you've found your Universal Assignment? You come alive. You resonate and vibrate with an internal "buzz." You become engaged, passionate, and hungry to make a difference. Gil Bailie, author of *Violence Unveiled: Humanity at the Crossroads*, said, "What the world needs are people who have come alive!" When you're alive, your positive energy is contagious. The world knows you're on a mission.

Sometimes, if we're not careful, we can find ourselves following the "wrong" Universal Assignment. Perhaps we heard about someone else's assignment, thought it sounded better than ours (more noble, more interesting, more exciting, more rewarding), and decided to "borrow" it. Or maybe we've allowed ourselves to be influenced by someone else's ideas and opinions and created a purpose designed to please that other person. Either way, we're living an assignment that was never meant for us. If you pay close attention, you'll begin to notice that something in your life doesn't feel right—you don't feel comfortable in your own skin. If that's the case, I invite you to commit to being authentic and to creating the life you were meant to have. Until you recognize your genuine Universal Assignment, your diamond brilliance can't shine through.

The following Personal Appraisal exercise is a *starting*

point in your quest to uncover your Universal Assignment. Understand that after completing it, you may not yet clearly see your purpose. That's okay . . . it *will* come. You are embarking on a journey of discovery, to unearth the brilliant diamond you were meant to be. Continue reading . . . continue digging for the genius that lies within you. The Personal Appraisal questions and exercises in subsequent chapters, the stories of Living Diamonds, and the Diamond Polishing action steps have been carefully designed to help you do deep inner work. When you've finished reading this entire book, come back and revisit this exercise. I believe you'll be inspired by the clarity you will have gained.

If you haven't already done so, I want to strongly urge you to find a Brilliandeer, an Accountability Partner who will help you stay the course and not feel alone in this process. This will further strengthen, sustain, and support you on the path to brilliant living.

EXERCISE: *Discover Your Universal Assignment*

1. Use the questions under Internal Buzz (at the top of p. 35) and External Need (at the bottom of p. 35) as thought starters and jot down some notes for each.
2. Look for connections between the items under both Internal Buzz and External Need.
3. Use those connections—the intersection of your genius and the needs of the world—to begin to draft your Universal Assignment (in the middle of p. 35).

1. INTERNAL BUZZ
- What activities make me feel alive?
- What do people tell me I'm good at?
- What are my special talents, skills, and abilities?

_____

_____

_____

_____

_____

3. INTERSECTION–YOUR UNIVERSAL ASSIGNMENT
- What would I do if I knew I couldn't fail?
- How can I add value to another life or to society at large?
- What am I here to do?

_____

_____

_____

_____

_____

2. EXTERNAL NEED
- What do I want to do?
- What external problems, situations, or needs nag at me?
- What opportunities, careers, or vocations am I interested in but haven't pursued?

_____

_____

_____

_____

_____

Discovering your Universal Assignment is crucial, but truth be told, it is just the first step on your journey to releasing your brilliance. You've already started by asking a big, soul-searching question: "Why am I here?" If you can believe it, the next question is even bigger: "Now that I know why I'm here, how am I supposed to live out my assignment each day?"

The answer: *You have to make a conscious decision to design your life around your Universal Assignment.* Your mission while you are here on Earth is to release your brilliance through your Universal Assignment. Your assignment should be something concrete. It's not a dream, but a fixed, compelling goal that drives your decisions, actions, and life choices. *Frankenstein* author Mary Shelley said, "Nothing contributes so much to tranquilize the mind as a steady purpose—a point on which the soul may fix its intellectual eye."

You're probably thinking, "That's great, Simon, but how exactly do I design my life around my Universal Assignment?" Good question! You need to **A.S.K.**:

ASK

Every day, ask this question: "How can I use my Universal Assignment to make a difference?" As soon as you ask the question, you open your subconscious mind to the possibilities. Unfortunately, many people who discover their Universal Assignment never take that next step—they never make the effort to plan their life around it. As a result, they continue to plod along through the same mundane, mediocre life. In many ways, these people are worse off than those who never recognize their purpose, because they know they have so much to contribute, and yet they settle for less than they could be.

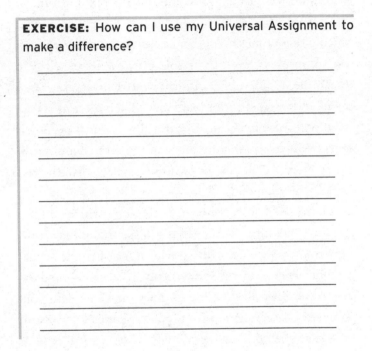

EXERCISE: How can I use my Universal Assignment to make a difference?

SEEK

Actively look for answers to how you can use your Universal Assignment each day. Find the path that you're supposed to take. Do some research if necessary. Understand that you may have to follow a lot of rabbit trails, some of which will take you to dead ends. That's okay; it's part of the process. The path to living out your Universal Assignment isn't always obvious and clear cut.

Seek the guidance of people who can help you live your assignment. Some people *pass through* your life, and others *come into* your life. Those who pass through will intersect with your life at a specific point in time or during a particular event. Be open to those who appear during these times. Whether or not you or they know it on a conscious level, their sole purpose is to help you reach the next level of fulfilling your Universal Assignment and releasing your brilliance. Then there are those who will come into your life and stay for a while. Their purpose is to continually push you to stretch and grow. They are the Brilliandeers who will help polish the facets of your diamond.

Learn to identify who in your life is which kind of person, and appreciate both types for the unique function they serve in your life. Just as it is not your purpose to touch *everyone*, the same is true in reverse. You don't need everyone in your life to help you complete your Universal Assignment, just a few someones. *If everyone will reach just one*, the world will be chock-full of blazingly brilliant diamonds.

EXERCISE: *Seek Guidance*

People Who Have Passed Through My Life	What I Learned from Them

People Who Have Come into My Life and Stayed	Their Ongoing Purpose in My Life

KNOCK

When you come upon a door of opportunity that you intuitively believe is for you, you've got to knock! And if you want to find out what's on the other side of that door, you're going to have to push it open and step through. Be open to the possibilities of your life. When they appear, be ready to take advantage of them.

Every single day, take one small step that moves you in the direction of your purpose. Believe within your spirit that this is why you're here. Make the decisions and choices that will bring into your life the things that will help you fulfill your assignment. Will you always know which is the right choice? No. Sometimes you'll just have to go with the flow. But with each decision and each step, you'll learn something that you can take with you and apply to the next experience. Each step you take accelerates your learning. Each step builds your faith, belief, and momentum.

Follow these three steps, purposefully and consciously, every day, day in and day out. If you do, I promise that you'll wake up one day just a few short years from now and your life will be completely transformed. You will be living your Universal Assignment and releasing your brilliance. When you A.S.K., the universe responds. As you ask, seek, and knock on doors, a series of synchronistic events begins to unfold. And the more you A.S.K., the more confident you'll become about the next step.

Sound like hype? I challenge you to do it and prove me wrong!

Perhaps you've already discovered your Universal Assignment, and you're well on the way to living it every day. If so, I invite you to do two things: First, revisit your purpose. Your assignment often changes as you change. Does it still resonate with you? Have you developed new skills, acquired more knowledge, or experienced profound life lessons that could bring more insight to your purpose? Many years ago, diamonds were often cut right at the mine where they were discovered. Mine-cut diamonds are beautiful and valuable in their own right because of their uniqueness and rarity. But it's common for owners of these old-fashioned cut diamonds to have them recut to increase their value and maximize their brilliance. If you've known of your Universal Assignment for a while, you undoubtedly have already made a valuable contribution. And yet, I would like you to consider re-evaluating your assignment and recutting the diamond that is you so that you might shine even brighter.

Second, in addition to your Universal Assignment, you now have another assignment—from me. And that is to help others find their Universal Assignments. Walk along beside them as a coach and friend and invite them to look at themselves in the mirror of life. Guide others to the place where they will ask, "Who do I want to be? How do I want to leave my mark?" But heed this warning: Sometimes, people who have found their Universal Assignment are so alive with it that they inadvertently try to force their own assignment on everyone else. Release the need to be right, and let others follow their own journey.

When you know your Universal Assignment and

design your life around it, your brilliance is released to the world. You become engaged, passionate, and hungry to be different and make a difference. You become an "infuser"—someone who fills others with energy, inspiration, and hope. When you do what you were born to do, you enter into a rhythm where everything connects. You discover the Law of Least Effort, when living, being, doing, and having become effortless. You no longer have to try so hard, and you experience less tension and anxiety.

As you use your Universal Assignment to release your brilliance, you create a legacy and, at the same time, become a role model for children (your own and others') who will one day want to leave their own legacy. The greatest gift you can leave the next generation is a good name. The book of Proverbs says, "A good name is more desirable than great riches." As you fulfill your Universal Assignment, you become known as a person with a purpose, as someone who makes a difference in the lives of others.

Remember, you are given only a certain amount of time to make your mark here on Earth. What will it be?

A LIVING DIAMOND:
A Real-Life Story from Mary

Ever since I was a young child, I knew that I enjoyed "coaching" people and helping them have more fun in life. As a member of the swim team, I loved working with the younger kids and making the older ones laugh.

I was both ringleader and cheerleader. In college, I discovered that I have a creative gift as well as a talent for seeing the unique side of things. I also found that I love motivating people, and I gravitated to the "celebrities" on campus such as Bo Jackson and Charles Barkley, sports heroes at Auburn.

Finding my Universal Assignment, however, wasn't a simple matter of discovering I had these gifts and putting them all together. I knew I had something to offer the workforce, but didn't know how or where it would play out. Understanding my purpose has been a journey with many twists and turns that has taken me all over the country and through numerous careers—some of them wonderful, others not so pleasant. I've worked everywhere from Capitol Hill to Wall Street, and I've experienced a truly vast array of professions, including celebrity-lecture agent, publicist, business coach, corporate trainer, speaking coach, reporter, news anchor, and TV personality.

But, as I discovered, one's Universal Assignment is about far more than just a career. Becoming a mother gave me another glimpse of my purpose and moved me one step closer to my Universal Assignment. It wasn't until our family hit rock bottom from the cumulative effects of my son's medical issues, a move, and a business buyout that I found the last piece of the puzzle. Every resource, every ounce of energy, and every thought went into just surviving. That was the first time I ever had to really struggle in life. I realized that life can hit anyone hard, at any time, and that the strength you build while fighting your way back will make you incredibly strong and powerful. The quality of genuine compassion that I gained from that experience I believe has made me truly a masterful coach.

Now I know that my Universal Assignment is to nurture others, to help them grow and blossom into strong, confident people. I work as a coach to leaders in major corporations, guiding them to deliver true value to their organizations. I also know that my gifts are being used and my purpose is being fulfilled through my roles as a mother and a wife. I finally feel that all of my strengths have come together and that I'm the only person in the world who can do what I do, the way I do it. My confidence shines through, and I feel a sense of inner peace. My "work" is effortless and fun.

Although not all of my personal dreams have yet come to fruition, I can now see that I had to grow into my Universal Assignment. I had to live through the highs and lows of life and gain a lot of education, training, and experience to finally come to the place where I have the talent, skills, and wisdom to use my gifts to serve the world. It was a process, not an overnight achievement. And while I wouldn't want to go back and relive all the pain I've endured, I'm thankful for those experiences because they were integral in shaping me into a woman who can live my purpose with passion.

PERSONAL APPRAISAL

I invite you to answer the following questions:

1. Are you living your Universal Assignment? If not, why not?
2. Examine your life and identify opportunities that have

presented themselves to you. Did you walk through the door, take advantage of them, and move forward into your brilliance, or did you slam the door shut and withdraw? What can you learn from these experiences? What opportunities are presenting themselves to you *right now*? Are you prepared to take advantage of them?

3. How can you proactively create your own opportunities to fulfill your Universal Assignment?

DIAMOND POLISHING

Here are three action steps you can take to polish your facets and discover and fulfill your Universal Assignment:

1. Decide today to actively seek your Universal Assignment. Then, every day, declare and affirm that you are making a contribution and living a brilliant life.
2. Identify three "doors of opportunity" on which you should be knocking.
3. Once you are satisfied with your Universal Assignment, decide how you can help three other people discover their Universal Assignments.

♦ Visit www.ReleasingBrilliance.com for more resources, exercises, tips, and tools for discovering your Universal Assignment.

A GEM FOR YOU

Your Universal Assignment is not to touch everyone, it is to touch someone.

FACET: PIQUE YOUR CURIOSITY

"BUT DESIRE OF KNOWLEDGE, LIKE THE THIRST OF RICHES,
INCREASES EVER WITH THE ACQUISITION OF IT."

–LAURENCE STERNE, AUTHOR OF *THE LIFE AND OPINIONS OF
TRISTRAM SHANDY, GENTLEMAN*

Do you remember Curious George? He's the inquisitive little monkey who, along with his friend The Man with the Yellow Hat, stars in the *Curious George* children's books by Margaret and H. A. Rey. George observes everything that goes on around him. And because he's curious, he wants to investigate unfamiliar things and experience new situations for himself. Can he make a pizza? Be a lifeguard? Ride a bicycle? Lead the parade? You can bet he's going to find out! George is a risk taker. His curiosity compels him to jump in with all four feet and live life to the fullest. Sometimes he's scared, and sometimes his inquisitive nature creates chaos or gets him into sticky situations. But in the end, he always saves the day and learns something new and valuable in the process.

Can a children's-book character actually be a good role model for adults? Can a monkey teach us something about releasing our brilliance? Absolutely!

Curiosity is a desire to know or learn. Never underestimate the power of curiosity. Whether or not you realize it, your mind thrives and comes alive when faced with a challenge. You allow your brilliance to be released when you admit that you don't know something but are eager to find out about it. When you make it your personal goal to investigate the world around you, that desire to know becomes an inner drive to discover the new in the old and the old in the new. The magic in curiosity is unraveling a mystery and solving a riddle.

Inquisitive people ask questions, seek answers, wonder how things work, and try fresh approaches to old problems. You can easily recognize them by their behaviors.

- **Curious people are constantly searching for "new" information.** You'll find them in bookstores and libraries, sitting on the floor, absorbed in a book about some seemingly random subject. They proactively solicit feedback from their managers, spouses, friends, and coworkers. They ask profound and insightful questions—questions that cause you to stop and say, "Hmmm," and ponder a while. If you're still accessing the same information you were five or ten years ago, how much has your knowledge bandwidth increased? Strive to continually search for new knowledge, whether it's by reading books, talking to people, or pursuing other means.

- **Curious people are doers and teachers.** Instead of waiting to be told to do something, they do it and ask permission later. They know that the more they practice and teach a concept the more meaningful it becomes. One way I remember new ideas is to start talking about them! I immediately tell someone else about what I've learned, expanding the concept and taking it deeper. This gives me the opportunity to solidify the thought in my mind and link it to established concepts and to share that same fresh idea with others right from the start.

- **Curious people don't just hear, they listen.** (Hearing is a physical function; listening is an intellectual function.) They are truly interested in and intrigued by what the other person is saying. Listening requires you to tune in all your frequencies to the person speaking so that you not only hear the message, but also see the nonverbal cues, feel the speaker's emotion, and catch the deeper meaning behind the words. The next time someone else is talking to you, practice *listening*.

Curiosity naturally leads you to learn, unlearn, and re-learn. Philosopher Eric Hoffer says, "In the future, the learners will inherit the earth, while the learned will find themselves beautifully equipped to live in a world that no longer exists." As if to prove his point, the managing executives of Japan's Sony Corporation have a policy of disregarding every employee's educational qualifications after he or she is hired. They want every individual to be seen as an achiever, an innovator, a "seeker of the unknown" in contributing to building a better world, and not be judged by their academic achievements alone.

In the future, the business compensation model will value knowledge over activity. If you're a curious person with a mind that's geared toward finding solutions, you will always be in demand, and you will be able to work for the organization of your choice. Your knowledge will set you apart in a crowd of highly talented, motivated people.

A LIVING DIAMOND:
A Real-Life Story from Randi

You could probably call me a "perpetual learner," not to be confused with a "perpetual student." I don't like that uncomfortable feeling you get when you're bored with yourself and feel stale. The exploration of new information is a "rush" for me.

Learning is more than just showing up and listening. I think the gift is in the curiosity—the need to know more and then take what is learned and put it to work, sometimes in unexpected ways. The subject doesn't really matter—it could be calculus or knitting. It's the process of learning that's important. The setting doesn't have to be in a classroom. The teacher can be a book, a friend, a trip, an audiotape, or a software program. The process can be as simple as allowing yourself solitude to think, review, and analyze things differently. Or it can be lengthy, with stops and starts, and then a look back filled with pride at what you've accomplished.

My career in the financial services arena lasted nineteen years until industry downsizing caught up with me. Fortunately, I had a number of options because I had developed transferable knowledge and skills through involvement in professional organizations. Those skills helped me move forward again in my career. My goal was always to learn more, not necessarily to grab a promotion or a better position. Some people do the same job in the same way for years. In today's workplace, that's dangerous. Change easily outpaces us. If you don't continually learn, you may become unqualified for your job.

A few months after I started a job in a new field, I attended a workshop. There I was exposed to new ideas! I was captivated by the information and suddenly felt like I had found a part of myself that had been, if not lost, at least overlooked. There was that "aha!" moment during the seminar when my body and brain both wanted to dance. My mind raced, thinking of ways I could use this information. I realized for the first time how important it was for me to challenge myself intellectually.

My mother once told me I'd better find a man and get married because I'd never make it on my own. Imagine how I felt when my brief marriage ended in divorce! Being on my own, I've learned to do simple home repairs,

install molding, hang curtain rods, paint, stencil, clean
out the dryer vent on the roof, and plant the landscaping.
One promise I made to myself was that I would not stay
home just because I didn't have someone to travel with.
Now, traveling alone is one of my greatest joys! I love to
rent a car and just go exploring.

In life, we have to set our own goals and celebrate
our own victories—even if no one else notices. What a
wonderful feeling of accomplishment it is when you
learn a new skill, absorb new information, conquer a
fear, or try something new!

Get curious about learning! *How* you learn is just as
important as, if not more important than, *what* you learn.
You might start by investing in a copy of *The Learning
Revolution* by Gordon Dryden and Jeannette Vos. It's a
big book featuring a lifelong learning system that you
might have to read several times, but once you "get it,"
your life will never be the same. I suggest paying particular attention to the discussion of Harvard University professor Howard Gardner's innovative theory of multiple
intelligences. Gardner's philosophy is that the traditional
IQ-based measure of intelligence is too limited. Instead,
he suggests there are eight different kinds of intelligence
that better represent the broad range of potential that exists within each of us. The eight types of intelligence are

- Linguistic — word smart
- Logical/mathematical — reasoning/number smart

- Spatial – visual/picture smart
- Kinesthetic – body smart
- Musical – music smart
- Interpersonal – people/social smart
- Intrapersonal – intuitive/self smart
- Naturalist – nature smart

Your intelligence is the area in which you thrive. It's what comes naturally to you. When you use your unique intelligence, you feel fulfilled and engaged. Just as a diamond shines the brightest when it is cut to the shape of its natural profile (such as emerald, pear, or marquise), you will most easily release your brilliance when you operate in your natural intelligence.

In college I thought I wanted to be an accountant. It didn't seem to matter that I hated math! One day, a professor who had seen me speak in front of a large group said to me, "Don't be an accountant—that's not who you are. You thrive in public speaking. Save yourself some agony and grief. Stop pursuing accounting and do what you love." That was when I stepped back and took some time to discover that my intelligence is linguistic. Pursuing endeavors like speaking and writing, which draw on my natural intelligence, has provided me with a great income, a nice lifestyle, and most important, an outlet to express my brilliance.

I strongly encourage you to identify your natural intelligences, then invest in them and learn how to leverage them. Take classes and attend workshops and seminars on how to develop your natural inclinations.

Seek out professional development organizations that feed your intelligence and your curiosity. Search the web. Ask other people with the same natural intelligence as you, "How do I become the best in this area?"

When you know which of the eight is your type of intelligence, learning and discovery become fun. You learn because you want to, not because you have to. You're excited to see what else you can discover, and you're ready to jump into new situations with both feet. You become a risk taker, willing to experience life to the fullest.

Sounds like a certain little monkey I know.

PERSONAL APPRAISAL
I invite you to answer the following questions:

1. What are your natural intelligences? Rank the intelligences below (based on Howard Gardner's theory of multiple intelligences) in order from 1 to 8, with 1 being your strongest intelligence and 8 being your weakest.

INTELLIGENCE	RANK
Linguistic *(word smart)*	_____
Logical/mathematical *(reasoning/number smart)*	_____
Spatial *(visual/picture smart)*	_____
Kinesthetic *(body smart)*	_____
Musical *(music smart)*	_____
Interpersonal *(people/social smart)*	_____
Intrapersonal *(intuitive/self smart)*	_____
Naturalist *(nature smart)*	_____

2. What is your primary learning style (auditory, visual, kinesthetic)?
3. Are you curious enough to stretch your thinking capacity and skill set?

DIAMOND POLISHING

Here are three action steps you can take to polish your facets and foster your curiosity.

1. Start asking bigger questions. For example, "How much value can I create using my intelligence?" or "How can I use my three strongest intelligences to further my Universal Assignment and release my brilliance?"
2. Find opportunities to teach what you've learned to others to help awaken their curiosity.
3. Every day this week, list three things you're curious about, whether or not you think they're important. These could be anything from "How do traffic lights work?" to "How does my boss make decisions?" This exercise will increase your curiosity quotient. (Make sure you find the answers!)

A GEM FOR YOU

You release your diamond brilliance when you operate in your natural intelligence.

PART TWO

RELEASE YOUR BRILLIANCE

> **"YOUR FUTURE IS CREATED BY WHAT YOU
> DO TODAY, NOT TOMORROW."**
>
> **−ROBERT KIYOSAKI, ENTREPRENEUR**

Diamonds are valuable because of their unique physical and chemical properties. And yet diamonds are just carbon in its most concentrated form. That's it—carbon, one of the most common elements in the world and a fundamental building block of all living organisms. Did you know the human body is 18 percent carbon?

Carbon is the same element that makes up graphite, a common substance (think pencil lead) with properties *very* different from diamond. Diamond is the hardest mineral known to man; graphite is one of the softest. Diamond is transparent; graphite is opaque. Diamond is an excellent electrical insulator; graphite is a good conductor of electricity.

How can two materials with exactly the same chemical composition be so different? Why are diamonds uncommon, while carbon is so common? Natural diamond can be formed only under intense heat and pressure hundreds of miles below the earth's surface. For a diamond to be created, carbon must be placed under pressure (45,000 to 60,000 times our everyday atmospheric pressure), at temperatures between 900 and 1,300 degrees Celsius. At lower pressures or temperatures—and at higher temperatures—graphite is formed instead of diamond. In other words, the conditions must be just right to create a diamond.

Likewise, if all of us are born with the same "composition"—with the source of brilliance already within us—why do some people shine brilliantly while others are dull? Why do some become diamonds and others remain common graphite?

When I was growing up, my mom would always say, "You are a product of your environment." As you mature, you are shaped by different aspects of your environment: your family life, your education, your relationships, your positive and negative experiences, and the people who influence you in some way. As an adult, your environment continues to mold you. The people around you help shape your opinions and decisions. Under the best possible circumstances, you would live, work, and play in an environment where you're nurtured, encouraged, and challenged . . . one where you are celebrated rather than just tolerated. In an environment like that, it will be much easier to release your brilliance.

But ultimately, and thankfully, environment is not the determining factor in whether or not you will become the diamond you were intended to be. I am here to tell you that *you can overcome your environment*. You can rise above the negative effects of destructive, damaging events and experiences.

A LIVING DIAMOND:
A Real-Life Story from Paulo

Many years ago, a friend told me that I live life like I'm going to die tomorrow. I smiled and simply said, "You seem to live your life like you will never die."

Brilliance lies in understanding the fact that we are born and we will die and realizing that what counts in life is what we do while we are alive. We are not candles in the wind—we have the power to control the wind and the fire.

My family was the reason I woke up to life. Coming from a family with twenty-one siblings, I desperately wanted to help my parents. My father was sick, but worked day and night. As a boy, I promised myself I would help him to have a better life.

I had a whole life in front of me, but my father was already old. So, when I was thirteen years old, I began a race against time. My vision was simple: If I wanted to win in life, I knew I'd have to study, I'd have to educate myself, and I'd have to run faster than anybody else. I sacrificed my nights and weekends to reach my goals. Nothing could erase from my memory the sight of my dad waking up at 3:00 A.M., going to work, and often not returning home until midnight. But I accepted that memory as a gift from God, because although it might have created sadness for some people, for me it was inspiration to keep moving faster. If you want to be brilliant, you must find passion in what you do, or you won't have the energy you need to reach the sky.

I made my dream come true. I was (am) able to help my parents and my family. My father is in Heaven now. I know as I write these lines, he is present beside me and proud of his little boy.

My philosophy about life is this: The man who moves a mountain is the one who carries it stone by stone. Modern culture tries to convince people they can move mountains overnight. Not me. I keep at it the old-fashioned way—moving my mountains stone by stone, day and night, while some people sleep, while others make fun of me. That is how I accomplished all my dreams yesterday; that is how I keep moving mountains today; and that is how I will move the world tomorrow.

There are countless stories of people who triumphed over seemingly insurmountable odds to achieve personal and professional success. How did they do it? They took control of their thoughts, beliefs, and actions. *Diamond people understand the connection between thoughts, beliefs, actions, and outcomes.* Martin E. P. Seligman explains it this way: Our reaction to each experience, conversation, or situation we encounter is to think about it. These thoughts rapidly congeal into beliefs. These beliefs can become so habitual that we don't even realize we have them unless we stop to focus on them. And they don't just sit there idly; they have consequences. Our beliefs directly influence what we feel and what we do. They can mean the difference between feeling dejected and giving up on the one hand and feeling optimistic and taking constructive action on the other. And of course, our actions—or our inactions—have a direct and profound impact on our results.

Your thoughts, beliefs, and actions represent the combination to the vault where your diamond potential is kept. These are the critical factors that will release the brilliance that exists within you, and consequently, determine the quality of your life.

Any jeweler will tell you that diamonds are described using The Four C's: clarity, color, cut, and carat. The first three—clarity, color, and cut—are the factors that determine a diamond's quality, its beauty, and how brilliantly it will shine. As such, they are a powerful analogy for the first three steps toward releasing your brilliance. Carat is a measure of diamond weight, and although it doesn't affect the quality of a stone, it is a key factor in the overall value of a diamond. Likewise, carat is the crucial fourth step in your transformational process.

Clarity, a measure of a diamond's purity, represents your thoughts—your profound insights into who you are and why you do what you do. A diamond's magical color represents your beliefs about yourself and the world around you. Cut symbolizes action: A diamond will forever remain a rough stone unless the cutter acts on it. Likewise, your brilliance will remain locked in the vault unless you take specific action. When your thoughts, beliefs, and actions are directed and integrated, your brilliance is released to the world.

Part II takes an in-depth look at these three critical factors and explains how they operate in your everyday life. You will uncover the key principles, or facets, that you must practice and polish. Soon, you will discover your authentic self and your authentic relationships. You will focus your talents and energies on what matters most. And you will engage your heart and mind to grow, and as a result, become more engaged in your life.

A Gem for You

Diamond people understand the connection between thoughts, beliefs, actions, and outcomes.

CLARITY: SEEK PROFOUND INSIGHT

Clarity is possibly the most important factor affecting the quality and value of any diamond. Clarity literally means "clearness" and refers to a diamond's ability to allow the free passage of light. Extremes of clarity can produce a brilliant, magnificent diamond or a cloudy, dull, and lifeless stone. Most diamonds have natural imperfections, called inclusions, that affect the clarity by stopping light from passing through the stone. Inclusions look like tiny crystals, clouds, spots, or feathers and are unique to every diamond. Some people don't see inclusions as flaws, but rather as identifying characteristics, or "nature's fingerprints." The clarity of a diamond is graded by how many, how big, and how visible the inclusions are—the fewer and smaller the inclusions, the more valuable the diamond.

As people, we all have "inclusions"—none of us is perfect. It is necessary for each of us to identify our personal inclusions in the journey toward understanding our own value. No matter where you start in life, you will never be perfect. Guess what? It's okay. Just recognize the need to do the inner work. A flawless diamond with perfect clarity is extremely rare. And in most other diamonds, the imperfections are so small that they have minimal effect on the beauty and brilliance of the stone. Your goal is not perfection; your goal is to discover "nature's fingerprints" on your life. Once you clearly see your inclusions, you can take action to minimize them and increase your internal and external value.

Much like a jeweler who uses a magnifying loupe to evaluate a diamond for clarity, you must focus on your life and use profound insight to evaluate where you are in life and what your motives are. Profound insight is about gaining a fresh perspective by suspending old thinking patterns and seeing the new in the old. When we step outside our habitual thinking patterns, we experience what Peter Senge, author of *The Fifth Discipline*, calls "profound disorientation," in which the ways we see and make sense of the world come unglued. Often in this state of disorientation, the light switches on in our brains, and we discover new ways to view, interpret, and think about ourselves and how we relate to the world around us. In these defining moments of enlightenment, you suddenly understand what needs to be done. But until you slow down to the speed of thought and reflect on why you think the way you do, you're just skimming the surface, and you'll never gain complete clarity.

Profound insight leads to clear thinking or clarity about who you are. Clarity embraces the inclusions of self-limitation, while grasping for the authentic truth. Clarity allows you to tap into your innate wisdom and stay emotionally aligned. Clarity is the first step toward creating your future and living your brilliance.

A GEM FOR YOU
Your goal is to discover "nature's fingerprints" on your life.

FACET: EXAMINE YOUR MOTIVES

"LET IT BE YOUR CONSTANT METHOD TO LOOK INTO
THE DESIGN OF PEOPLE'S ACTIONS, AND SEE WHAT
THEY WOULD BE AT, AS OFTEN AS IT IS PRACTICABLE;
AND TO MAKE THIS CUSTOM THE MORE SIGNIFICANT,
PRACTICE IT FIRST UPON YOURSELF."

—MARCUS AURELIUS, ROMAN EMPEROR

Lorraine worked as an executive assistant for a CEO who didn't value his employees. In fact, he was often downright abusive. Most exchanges with him were unpleasant, but Lorraine still tried to be a productive employee. One day, as the CEO was leaving for an important trip, she noticed he had forgotten some crucial documents. She decided not to make him aware of it, fearing he might reprimand her for helping him. In that moment, she knew it was time to find another job. She realized her motive was no longer top performance, but self-preservation. This was a moment of truth for her, and shortly thereafter, she found another job where her employer valued her.

Moments of truth often reveal the motives of your heart. If your motives are pure and honest, you will experience forward momentum. If they're not, your brilliance will remain locked up. Let me give you a personal example.

A decade ago, when I relocated to Orlando, Florida, I made a list of the key leaders in this emerging city. These were the men and women whose names carried enough weight to open doors and close deals. My goal was to leverage their community status and gain access to their Rolodexes of movers and shakers.

Were my motives pure? No. Needless to say, I never met them when I wanted to because I was always trying to control the situation so they would perceive me a certain way. I showed up at every event like Johnny-on-the-spot, trying to be seen and heard, but never connecting with people because they could sense my cunning motives a mile away.

Now, you're probably wondering how I managed to change my course. I began working with a life coach who saw right through me. He immediately recognized my performance-driven behaviors as my need for external validation in order to feel confident. How I felt about myself, and therefore my motives, depended on what others thought of me. When validation comes from within, however, it's permanent and real. Your confidence can't be shaken by the way others react to you. Authentic confidence leads to authentic motives, which are sensed by those around you, thus creating an authentic connection and authentic results.

For example, do you have friends who live in an up-scale neighborhood who are constantly reminding you of their prestige? Do they talk about living next door to So and So who has blue blood or works for a blue-chip company? Are their motives wrapped up in the net worth of the neighborhood or in the relationship wealth of the neighborhood? How do you feel when you talk with these people? Do you feel an authentic connection, as if they truly care about you? Or do they seem more concerned about what they will gain from their rela-tionship with you?

How often have you heard the phrase "Go for the money"? Perhaps you, or someone you know, have been offered a job with a significant pay increase, and the motivation to take it was purely monetary. There wasn't much consideration given to whether the job itself was a good fit, let alone the organization's mission, values, or people philosophies. So you took the job, only to dis-cover there was a good reason it paid more money: The work environment was unpleasant, or there were a num-ber of unsavory problems to deal with. The company had to pay more just to keep employees around.

Don't misunderstand me. There's nothing wrong with a hefty paycheck or living in an upscale neighbor-hood. But beware if money or prestige is your primary motivation. Without a more heartfelt motivation, at the end of your life, you may be faced with a burning ques-tion: "Was it worth it?"

I invite you to do the inner work of examining your

motives, no matter what the situation. If you fail to
do so, you risk building your life on an unstable foundation. Rid your system of the toxic behavior of back-
stabbing, politicking, and controlling outcomes.
Today, consider living your life with detached intention. When you're obsessed with achieving a particular outcome, you're disconnected from your spirit. But
when you're aligned with your spirit and feel peace
that's not based on a specific outcome, you release
your brilliance, and you will actually attract what's in
your highest good.

A LIVING DIAMOND:
A Real-Life Story from Lauren

A few years ago, I reached a point in my life where I
was sick and tired of being sick and tired. I
constantly worried about the direction of my life. I
harbored ill feelings toward people who had hurt me in
the past. Finally, I drove myself to a nervous breakdown
and ended up in the hospital. No drugs or alcohol were
consumed to get me there. According to my doctor, I
had exhausted my brain into a delusional state.

After that experience, I knew I had to gain control of
my life, and I decided to revisit a seminar I'd attended a
few years earlier. This time, I "got" the lesson, and I
walked away a different person. The nature of the
lesson doesn't really matter. The point is that my
motives were different the second time around. Initially,

I was so consumed with making sure I learned "something big" that I didn't really listen and completely missed the lesson I was looking for.

Now, I do things because I love to do them—my mind is no longer consumed by having an attachment to the result or reward. I spend time with friends because I'm enthusiastic about our friendship. At work, I deal with my clients honestly, whether I make the sale or not, because I choose to live a life of integrity. I've forgiven the people who deeply hurt me because I choose to live a life free from anger.

I live a fully passionate life. I choose to have passion in everything I do—from loving my mother to cooking a meal for myself. Passion drives my decisions. If something or someone lacks passion, I stay away from that situation or person. I'm now able to look inward and focus on unleashing the very best in me. Instead of focusing on the destination, I focus on the journey.

It's interesting to note that *motive* is the root word for motivation. Oftentimes, organizations want me to come in and "motivate" their teams. The first thing I tell them is that I'm an inspirational catalyst, not a motivator. I can't motivate you or anyone else for that matter. Only *you* and your motives can motivate you.

Authentic motives, such as positively contributing to another's life or having meaningful relationships, produce better outcomes and results in the long run than performance-driven motives like money and prestige. When you've discovered your Universal Assignment and you've begun to reconnect with your brilliance, you naturally become more motivated.

Bestselling author John Maxwell tells a story about the legendary "Bear" Bryant, former coach of the Alabama Crimson Tide football team. During one critical game, his team was ahead by six points with just a minute and a half left in the game. They had the ball, and it looked as if they had the game won.

Coach Bryant sent in a running play to his quarterback, but the quarterback decided to surprise the other team—and Coach Bryant—by calling a pass play. So he went back and threw a pass. The other team's defensive cornerback, the fastest guy in the league, intercepted the ball and headed toward the goal line. Alabama was about to lose the game.

The terrified Alabama quarterback, who *knew* what he'd done and who was known for his good arm but not for his fast legs, took off after the cornerback and tackled him on the five yard line. He saved the game and Alabama won.

The opposing coach went up to Coach Bryant after the game and said, "I thought that quarterback was slow! How'd he catch my world-class sprinter?" Coach Bryant looked at him and said, "You have to understand. Your man was racing for six points. My man was racing for his life."

Examine your motives. Are you racing for six points, or are you racing for your life?

PERSONAL APPRAISAL

I invite you to answer the following questions:

1. When was the last time you examined your motives for doing something? What did you discover about yourself?
2. What motivates you to be your best? What are the drivers, or "payoffs," that you seek?
3. Are you working just to earn a paycheck, or are you investing your intellectual energy in creating solutions and adding value?

DIAMOND POLISHING

Here are three action steps you can take to polish your facets and examine your motives:

1. Identify your self-serving and performance-driven behavioral characteristics. Write them down.
2. Think about your reasons for wanting to get ahead in your organization. Are they all about what you can get out of it, or are they about creating value and solution-oriented results?
3. Examine your motive behind every e-mail you send out. For instance, is it really necessary to forward copies to everyone in the company? Are you doing it because those people need the information, or are you doing it to cover all your bases? Instead, get up from your desk or pick up the phone and talk directly to the person who needs the information.

♦ Visit www.ReleasingBrilliance.com for more resources, exercises, tips, and tools for examining your motives.

A GEM FOR YOU
When your motives are authentic, you attract what's in your highest good.

FACET: EVALUATE THE CORE AREAS OF YOUR LIFE

In July 1986, a rough diamond weighing 599 carats was discovered in South Africa. The enormous stone was named the Centenary Diamond, in honor of the hundredth anniversary of De Beers Consolidated Mines, which owned the mine where the stone was found. Because of the irregular shape of the rough stone, it was determined that only the most skilled craftsman would be able to reveal the diamond's beauty without ruining it. The man chosen to cut the stone was Gabi Tolkowsky.

For one whole year, while the right tools and technical conditions were created to cut the diamond, Tolkowsky examined and evaluated it. Using the most sophisticated electronic instruments, he gazed deep into the crystal structure. When later asked about his work on the Centenary, Tolkowsky described himself as being taken over by the diamond. There was not a fissure or crevice of the stone that he did not know intimately.

Together with a small select team, Tolkowsky took almost three years to transform the rough stone into the world's largest, most modern-cut, top-color, flawless diamond. When finished, the Centenary weighed 273 carats and had 247 facets. Although the diamond is truly priceless, it has reportedly been insured for $100 million.

Like the Centenary, you are a priceless diamond, and only the most skilled craftsman can reveal the brilliance that lies within you. Who is this master cutter? God. Certainly, you will do most of the work to discover and release your brilliance, and other people in your life will also help to shape and polish you. But God is the master cutter. Only He knows the divine plan—the shape and size of the diamond you will become.

If you truly desire to become the magnificent diamond God intends you to be, you must evaluate the eight core areas of your life, or your eight Crown Facets, as I call them. Evaluation is about doing the deeper work—examining and analyzing your life, as if with a jeweler's loupe, until you intimately know every detail, every nook and cranny. When you "put your truth on the table" and get real with yourself, you begin to have clarity. You can clearly see, perhaps for the first time, which aspects of your life are integral to your brilliance and which ones are unnecessary. Those that detract from your brilliance should be cut away. Those that enhance your brilliance should be further polished.

Taking an honest look at your life isn't always fun, but when you consider how much more brilliantly you'll shine, I think you'll agree it will be worth it. Today, I invite you to take the time to carefully evaluate the eight Crown Facets of your life: spiritual, family, career, emotional, mental, wellness, social, and financial.

Spiritual: How are you doing spiritually? Your spirit is the very essence of who you are, the core of your brilliance. And your essence is revealed day in and day out by how you treat yourself, talk to yourself, and think about yourself. People won't value what you are becoming until you value who you are already.

Are you happy and fulfilled with the direction of your life? What can you do to increase your happiness quotient? Are you making progress in living a purposeful life by design, or are you still living an accidental life by chance? When you think about who you are, where you're going, and what you intend to accomplish, what is it in your life that provides spiritual meaning?

Developing, cultivating, and protecting your spiritual self takes some effort. Reawaken your spirit and reconnect your head to your heart. When you do this, you will enter into a rhythm of universal alignment where your entire being—your head, heart, hands, ears, and mouth—are connected to your spiritual brilliance.

Family: Your family is much more than just your spouse and your children. Family includes parents and grandparents, brothers and sisters, aunts and uncles, cousins and, yes, even pets. These are people and animals who can enrich your life in ways you can't begin to imagine. How much quality time do you invest in your relationships with those you love and care about the most? Are they a top priority, or do they get the "leftovers" of your life? Do you have any relationships that need mending? If so, don't wait . . . take the initiative to reconnect with those people and resolve your differences.

Here's the deal: If you were to "check out" tomorrow, the company you work for would empty your desk, clean out your office, and send your belongings to your loved ones. Your position would be posted on the company's job board and the Internet within a few days. You may think of yourself as irreplaceable, but the hard truth is that you're an employee—valuable, but not irreplaceable. But to your family, you truly are irreplaceable. Build your life around the people who will be crying at your funeral. Don't neglect them because of a job or career. Make the most of your time with those who know you the best and appreciate your brilliance. Better yet, support them and help them release their brilliance.

Career: Does your current work fulfill you, or are you working only for the paycheck and benefits? I know you may find this hard to believe (I did at first!), but your profession should be fun and exciting.

Are you solving problems and creating value for your organization? Adding to your organization's bottom line adds to *your* bottom line. When was the last time you read your company's annual report? That information is crucial to understanding the strategic direction of the organization where you spend a sizeable chunk of your waking hours.

Are you eager to advance your career? If so, what are you doing about it? Allow me to let you in on a secret: It's not the HR department's responsibility to promote you or show you how to get ahead. It's up to you to create your own career path. Robert Barner, author of *Lifeboat Strategies: How to Keep Your Career Above Water During Tough Times—or Any Time*, says: "Today's employer cannot guarantee the stability and longevity of corporate career paths or the security of employees' jobs. As a result, career strategists realize they have to take the initiative in charting their own direction."

I am convinced that to survive in the workplace of the future, it will be crucial to do four things: take responsibility for yourself, remain nimble, keep a great attitude, and constantly learn new skills. This is true whether you are an employee, an executive, or a self-employed professional. Are you multidimensional in your career approach? Do you have diverse skills and talents you could use in another field if you suddenly found yourself unemployed? Become your own career strategist. Evaluate your situation and then take the next step to move your career to the next level.

Emotional: How you react to the experiences of your life—good and bad—can overshadow your brilliance. Are your emotions running the show, or are you firmly in control? When your emotional house is in disarray, you often can't think or act rationally. Are you honest with yourself and in your relationships? Are there situations in your life about which you're in denial?

Many of the challenges and struggles we face in life are the result of our own "baggage." People often turn to self-help resources, such as success seminars, motivational speakers, and personal development workshops, to help them overcome their issues and get back on track. Many of these are great programs that deliver life-changing messages and do, in fact, offer help.

Unfortunately, I meet many people who are "addicted"

to these self-improvement programs. They spend thousands of dollars and many years searching for the "one thing" that will change their lives. They enjoy the motivational rush they get when they discover a new concept or principle—could this be "the one"? And although they try to apply it to their lives, sadly, they rarely achieve lasting change. Why? Because they aren't willing to do the soul-searching, gut-wrenching, heart-rending work that is necessary to truly internalize the concepts and permanently change their lives.

The great motivational leaders of our time are brilliant men and women, but you can't change your life simply by being in their presence or by reading their books (including this one!). Nothing will change until *you* change—until you actually integrate their principles into your life. Are you willing to do the work, to face the enemy (ene-ME) within? If you want to get your emotional life in order, you have no choice but to haul out your personal suitcase of issues, painstakingly go through it, and get rid of the things that are weighing you down.

Mental: Do you want to know where you'll be five years from now? Look at the people you call your friends, the books you read, the CDs and tapes you listen to, and the way you spend your time. Why? Because these are the things that influence your thinking. Anything that feeds your mind—positively or negatively—affects how you think.

Everything you have in your life today is the result of the way you've thought in the past. Likewise, everything you will—or won't—have in the future will be the result of the way you think today. You make decisions based on your thoughts and beliefs. Those decisions lead to actions, which produce results. If you want to change your output, then you must change your input. To change your results, change your thinking.

Who has your ear? What kind of people are they? How do you spend your leisure time? What kind of books do you read? According to author Jim Rohn, "If you read one book every month about your industry, in ten years you'll have read 120 books. That will put you in the top one percent of your field." What major events in your life have influenced the way you think? Reprogram your thoughts by accepting and listening to only those sources that positively nourish your mind.

Wellness: When I worked in the hospitality industry, one of our internal slogans was "A dead guest is an unhappy guest!" So true! All kidding aside, the reality is that you have to take care of yourself. If you don't, who will? Your body is the engine of your life. Everything you put into it either helps the engine run better or causes it to deteriorate. And every engine has to be maintained. Are you getting regular checkups, exercising consistently, drinking enough water, and getting plenty of rest? If not, your engine may break down when you need it most. If wellness is not at the forefront of your personal development agenda, I can almost guarantee that one day you will hit the wall through burnout, illness, or possibly even premature death.

If you get the feeling that I'm trying to scare you, I

am! Recently, the doctor told me I was thirty pounds overweight and warned me to lose the weight or suffer the potential health consequences. The slim, trim man I *thought* I was felt shocked and embarrassed. I knew I couldn't fit into some of my pants and suits, but since the weight gain had been gradual, I hadn't realized I'd gained so much. You see, my version of doing pushups was to push up my chair closer to the table. Since that doctor's visit, I've implemented a "push back" program!

How about you? What part of your engine needs some attention? Do you have nagging symptoms that you're afraid to get checked out? Don't delay. Give your body the attention it deserves, and do it now!

Social: Is your life full and enriching? Do you spend your social time on the couch with the remote control or out in the world expanding your horizons? Despite what many people think, the social aspect of our lives is crucial because it allows us to put our lives in perspective. When we travel, experience other cultures, view magnificent art, and immerse ourselves in music, we are once again reminded that the world is bigger than we are.

Are you happy in your relationships? Who are your friends? How are *they* doing in each of the core areas? That's important to know because you either grow or wither in the context of your relationships. Proverbs says, "As iron sharpens iron, so one person sharpens the wits of another." Your friends either sharpen or dull your mind and your potential. Do you have friends who use phrases like these?

- "I don't have time."
- "I can't do it."
- "I tried that once, and it didn't work."
- "The company doesn't pay me enough."

People who routinely use this kind of negative language diminish their own brilliance as well as yours. Perhaps you need to critically evaluate who in your life are friends and who are acquaintances. Then, consider investing more time in friends and less time in acquaintances. Just a thought!

Financial: How are you doing financially? Is there too much month left at the end of your money, so to speak? Money represents your life's energy. What you do with your money determines what you do with your life. What are you doing to ensure your financial future is secure? Do you have a plan to create a financial legacy for future generations? Have you ever considered setting up your own foundation to support organizations that are making a difference in the world?

I suggest you invest some money and time in the following resources:

- *Six Steps to Financial Fitness* by Tony Bland will teach you how to survive the financial challenges of modern society.
- *Secrets of the Millionaire Mind* by T. Harv Eker will help you master the inner game of wealth.

- *Rich Dad, Poor Dad* by Robert Kiyosaki will challenge you to make money work for you instead of you working for money.

When all eight of these core areas are balanced, you operate from a place of wholeness, and you experience peace and happiness. On the other hand, areas that are out of balance will cause you stress and discomfort. If the crown facets on a diamond are misshapen or unbalanced, the diamond can't show its fire and light. The same is true for you. You can't expect to shine brightly if key aspects of your life are in trouble.

Generally speaking, how well you're doing in each area correlates to the amount of resources you invest in that area. You will shine more brilliantly in each area if you invest more—more energy, more time, more focus, more money. Remember, a healthy balance maximizes your diamond's brilliance.

PERSONAL APPRAISAL

I invite you to answer the following questions:

1. What negative influences in your life are holding you back and should be eliminated?
2. Who is your biggest supporter, and who is your biggest detractor?
3. What makes you shine more brilliantly in each of the eight core areas?

A LIVING DIAMOND:
A Real-Life Story from Abby

Not too long ago, I was depressed in my career. I had worked hard to finish my graduate degree, and yet I wasn't being recognized or rewarded for my achievements.

Slowly, the light started to come on. I began to realize that I was focusing only on my career and letting all the other wonderful parts of my life go unattended.

I needed a kick in the pants. After making a list of "What Makes Abby Tick," I couldn't believe all the fun I'd forgotten to have: reading, theater, musicals, scrapbooking, videos, journaling . . . the list went on and on. I also decided to try some new experiences: I'm taking a course to learn how to write for children, and I've become a mentor to a second grader.

Not all of these experiences have been easy. I struggle with the writing course, but the inspiration and ideas I receive from my time with my student are immense! And because I did what was for the greater good—mentoring—I found benefits in other areas of my life.

Now, I don't worry as much as I used to. I find I can accept life as it comes, as long as what I'm doing makes me happy and is for the greater good. If I take care of all the facets of my life and don't neglect one for the other, the Universe will work to let all the pieces fall into place.

DIAMOND POLISHING: BRILLIANCE
THROUGH BALANCE

The following Brilliance Through Balance exercise will help you quickly discover which areas, if any, are out of balance. I invite you to put your truth on the table: How well are you doing in each area relative to how well you *want* to be doing? For example, how is your family life now compared to the vision or goal you have for it? Rate yourself on each of the eight Crown Facets according to the scale below.

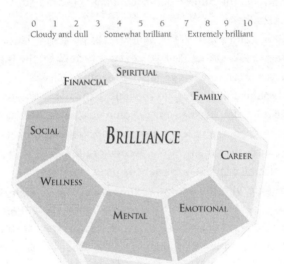

Now, review your scores. Overall, you're looking for relative balance among all eight areas and for higher, rather than lower, individual scores.

An ideal score is 8 or higher for each area, which indicates that you are well balanced and living your brilliance in all the key areas of your life. Any score between 6 and 8 indicates an area that needs some improvement. Write down some things you can do to tweak your thoughts, beliefs, and actions in this area.

Was there any aspect in which you scored 5 or lower? If so, this is probably an area where you already know there is a problem but aren't doing anything about it. Don't feel bad about a score of 5 or below—it's just a rough edge on the diamond that is you. The purpose of this exercise is to help you find the areas that need more polishing. Simply accept where you are, take responsibility for the situation, and take action to make it better.

For any area with a score of 5 or below, go back and reread the discussion on that topic earlier in this chapter. Answer the questions on paper and try to identify what specific challenges you're facing. Then talk with your Brilliandeer about possible steps you can take to improve. Finally, ask your Brilliandeer to help you set goals and hold you accountable for meeting those goals. For example, if you scored a 3 in Wellness, reread the Wellness section and identify the issue that is the most challenging for you. Is it your weight? Your blood pressure? Your cardiovascular health? Get a checkup, get some recommendations from your doctor, and then ask your Accountability Partner to help you put the doctor's recommendations into action.

A GEM FOR YOU

Once a year, evaluate the eight Crown
Facets of your life.

FACET: LIVE IN EMOTIONAL ALIGNMENT

Have you ever driven your car when it was out of alignment? Do you remember what it felt like? You probably didn't immediately notice that something was wrong. But as you drove, perhaps you felt a vibration or realized you had to work to keep the car from veering to one side.

Now, do you remember what it was like to drive the car after it was properly aligned? It was virtually effortless to keep the car straight on the road. Instead of having to grip the steering wheel with both hands, you could almost drive it with one finger. The shimmy was gone, and the ride was quiet and smooth.

As you travel down the road of life, you will move faster and with less effort if you are in emotional alignment. Emotional alignment keeps you moving forward on a straight heading even when you hit the inevitable potholes and bumps of life. Just as the wheels on your car need to be aligned to prevent wear and tear on the tires, your emotions need to be aligned to reduce the daily wear and tear of life and to prevent an emotional blowout or crash.

What does being in emotional alignment mean? It's living according to your values and principles. When you're in emotional alignment, *the way you feel on the inside matches the way you behave on the outside.* Your actions are in sync with your beliefs. You say what you mean. You're honest with yourself and in your relationships, and you communicate accordingly.

Conversely, when you're out of alignment, you're pulled in different directions; your heart tells you to do one thing, but your brain tells you to do another. There is a split in your soul, so to speak, because you're not living your life in harmony with your values. As a result, your energy is scattered and you feel drained. Burnout, toxic relationships, negative thoughts and self-talk, dishonesty with yourself and others—these are all signs that you are out of alignment.

Emotional misalignment is like an inclusion or flaw in the diamond that is You. Just as an inclusion stops the light from passing through a diamond, emotional misalignment affects your insight and clarity, prevents you from leveraging your gifts and talents, and diminishes your brilliance.

Have you ever been in a situation where some authority

figure asked you to do something you didn't feel comfortable doing? Maybe your boss asked you to pad the projections or misrepresent some information to someone. He or she probably assured you that it was "no big deal," that it was really in the best long-term interests of the company. And, because feeding your family is high on the priority list, you did it. However, your actions conflicted with your values of honesty and integrity, and so you felt very uncomfortable about it. That's because you were out of alignment. Did you feel like a brilliant diamond at that moment?

Every day, we face hundreds of choice points—moments when we must choose what we will do or how we will act. The choice we make determines whether we stay in alignment or move out of it. Will we choose to act based on our values, or will we bend to the will and desires of others? The more we choose to please others, the farther we move out of alignment.

These choice points happen frequently in all areas of our lives. Do we tell our spouses how much the shoes or the golf clubs really cost? How do we respond when a friend or co-worker asks for help? What excuse do we give ourselves for why we didn't exercise today? When the children ask if we have time to play a game with them, what do we say?

Every choice point is an opportunity to realign yourself with your inner truth. Ask yourself which choice matches your values. When you encounter situations that threaten to throw you out of alignment—the potholes of life—resist the temptation to ignore your internal compass. Stand up for what you believe. Push back. Make a decision based on your convictions. When you do, your diamond brilliance shines through.

When everything you feel, think, say, and do is in alignment, you enter into a flow, a rhythm. It's like being on cruise control. You move through life at an accelerated pace on the highway toward your brilliance. Consistent emotional alignment leads to emotional integrity—the state in which your internal alignment stays in place no matter what bumps or potholes you hit in life. It rejuvenates and reenergizes your spirit. It brings you to a place of clarity and keeps you focused so you can brilliantly shine.

PERSONAL APPRAISAL

I invite you to answer the following questions:

1. Are there specific behaviors you need to adopt in order to consistently live in emotional alignment?
2. Is there a split in your soul due to misalignment? If so, how do you plan to correct it?
3. What choices do you need to make today in order to live a brilliant life?

A LIVING DIAMOND:
A Real-Life Story from Madison

Someone hit the nail on the head with this observation about me: I live my life with an exclamation point! I've seen much success in my endeavors, both personal and business, and directly relate it to my energy, excitement, and enthusiastic approach to life. My passion is contagious, and it's genuine—not forced or fake. I think that shows.

Believing in myself, and I mean *truly* believing, is the key for me. Others may be thinner or more beautiful, but in my heart, I'm confident and self-assured. Give me a person who has average skills or looks, but who has heart and is self-assured, confident, and comfortable in his or her own skin, and you have a winner. People are naturally drawn to those who believe in themselves.

Almost four years ago, I left my job after twelve years with the same company. It was a *huge* leap of faith for me. I walked away from a job I deeply loved, was passionate about, and felt a great deal of pride and ownership in. But the time was right, and I knew this opportunity would never present itself in the same way again.

I left to start my own consulting business—to truly create something from the ground up that had never been done before. To my knowledge, I'm the only consultant in the country that specializes in my unique niche. The start was slower than I had anticipated, and there were indeed some nail-biting moments those first few years. But with the support of my loving husband, I soldiered on. We had to leverage quite a bit of equity we had built up in our home, but we were firm in our belief that there was a future in this initiative.

One by one, the clients started to come. Now, I turn down requests for consulting services on a weekly basis because there's simply not enough time to do it all. I travel all over the United States and the Caribbean speaking to large audiences. I was called on to work with two very high-profile clients: Billy Joel and Donald Trump. Those were experiences I will cherish for a lifetime and ones I *never* would have had if I'd taken the safer, easier road.

I've learned that we are all experts at whatever we do. But we must believe we're experts, and be bold enough to own our brilliance and share our knowledge, passion, and learning with no fear. That is what allows us to go to the next level in anything we do.

Today, my life is thrilling. I pinch myself every day. My job doesn't feel like work to me, and that makes getting up each morning so exciting.

People who know me often say I'm "lucky." I *am* lucky to have found a career that fulfills me and to have discovered it at such a young age. But I also know it took a lot of hard work. I love the quote "Luck is where preparation meets opportunity." We can't sit around and hope to get lucky. We have to plan to make remarkable things happen in our lives. We make our own luck.

Life is full of choices—hundreds of small choices each day plus a few big, life-altering decisions. I made the choice to go after my dreams and not wait for success to be handed to me. I chose to make my own destiny.

DIAMOND POLISHING

Here are three action steps you can take to polish your facets and live in emotional alignment.

1. Ask your Accountability Partner to give you feedback about how you behave on a regular basis. Are you more often in, or out of, alignment?
2. Write down three things you can do to live an emotionally aligned life on a daily basis.
3. Use every choice point in your life as an opportunity to check your emotional alignment.

♦ Visit www.ReleasingBrilliance.com for more resources, exercises, tips, and tools for living in emotional alignment.

A GEM FOR YOU

Every choice point is an opportunity to realign yourself with your inner truth.

COLOR: DISCOVER PURE, UNWAVERING BELIEF

"YOUR LEVEL OF BELIEF IN YOURSELF WILL INEVITABLY
MANIFEST ITSELF IN WHATEVER YOU DO."

—LES BROWN, MOTIVATIONAL SPEAKER

In nature, diamonds are found in a wide range of colors. We most often think of them being somewhere in the range between pure white (technically called colorless or transparent) and slightly yellow, but diamonds are also found in "fancy" colors, such as blues, greens, pinks, and even reds. A diamond acts like a prism, dividing light into the colors of the spectrum and then reflecting that light as colorful flashes called "fire."

A diamond's color is graded using a scale from D (colorless or pure white) to Z (light yellow). Like light passing through a clear glass window, more light passes through a completely colorless diamond than through a yellow-tinted one. Because pure white diamonds give off more sparkle and fire, the whiter the diamond, the higher the value.

What does pure white color represent in your diamond

life? Pure belief—belief in yourself and belief in your intuition. Do you have enough belief and confidence in who you are to live an authentic, transparent life? Or do you live an imposter's life because you're so filled with self-doubt that you're afraid to show the world who you truly are? Do you believe you can make a difference? Do you believe in your abilities? If so, then refrain from allowing your boat of confidence to be rocked by the waves of challenges, difficult circumstances, or changing expectations.

Pure white is also the color of faith. Faith is your belief in tomorrow when today is nothing short of chaos. Having faith in yourself protects your brilliance from other people's negativity.

How important is belief? Consider this: An experiment was conducted years ago to measure people's capacity to endure pain. Psychologists measured how long people could stand barefoot in a bucket of ice water. The researchers discovered there was one factor that made it possible for some people to stand in the ice water twice as long as others. Can you guess what that factor was?

Belief.

When the person in the ice water had a supporter, someone who believed in and encouraged him, he was able to endure the pain much longer than his unbelieving, unsupported counterparts. Those who withstood the incredible pain the longest were successful simply because they believed they would be.

What would the world be like if people heard on a regular basis that someone believed in them? Better yet, what would the world be like if each of us maintained an unwavering belief in ourself? Just think about it.

A diamond's color is permanent, unwavering. Constant, never-changing belief in yourself will lead to a brilliant, fiery life.

A Gem for You
Faith is your belief in tomorrow when today is nothing short of chaos.

FACET: IGNITE YOUR INTUITION

"INTUITION BECOMES INCREASINGLY VALUABLE
IN THE NEW INFORMATION SOCIETY PRECISELY
BECAUSE THERE IS SO MUCH DATA."

–JOHN NAISBITT, FUTURIST AND AUTHOR OF *MIND SET!*

Have you ever had an experience in which you just knew in your heart that something was—or wasn't—right? You couldn't necessarily explain how you knew; you just knew. That was your intuition.

Intuition is defined as knowing or sensing without the use of rational processes. In other words, intuition is knowing that surpasses your intellect! Call it a hunch, your sixth sense, or your intuitive intelligence. It's when you simply know you were meant to walk a certain path or make a specific decision. You don't know *why* you know, you just know.

Listening to and following your intuition is key to finding the combination that unlocks the vault where your brilliance is kept. Many people depend on hard data, schooling, logic, and experience to make decisions. And there's nothing wrong with that. However, I invite you to remain open to what your intuition might be telling you, especially if it's different from what the data or logic indicates.

There will also be times when you simply don't have enough information or data to make a good decision. What do you do then? Get quiet, listen to your gut, and then go with it.

Don't think I'm naïve enough to believe the world will simply accept your intuition at face value. "Feeling" is not a word used widely in business circles. I've sat in plenty of meetings over the years with skeptical colleagues who couldn't give a rip about anyone's hunches. They're more likely to say, "Show me the quantitative data" than "How do you feel about that?"

Going against the grain, especially in a corporate culture, may cause you to be labeled as a rebel. It isn't easy to follow your intuition instead of popular opinion or to question the rationale of a decision based on the data. But it's amazing to me that companies spend billions of dollars to acquire brilliant men and women, only to tell them, "Bring us your brains, but check your heart at the door."

When you make a decision based on your instincts, the world will either approve or disapprove. But in the end, you're the one who has to live with your decision.

How do you know when your intuition is on target? By the peace you'll have in your soul. Intuition is peace that surpasses all understanding. You feel at peace when you make decisions based on your inner knowing. Conversely, you will know a decision is not the right one if you feel discomfort or a nagging sense of unrest. Pay

A LIVING DIAMOND:
A Real-Life Story from Regina

I've been told I'm a "pragmatic visionary"—someone who can not only see the end result of a vision, but also design the steps to get there and attract the people to implement them. It's taken a lifetime (or twenty years, at least) to uncover this unique ability— a lifetime of experiences and sifting out the essence of each one. I've also had to follow the thread of intuition to connect with people who could show me how to better integrate my intuition with my cognitive mind in order to achieve heart-mind congruency.

Now, every day is a miracle rather than a mystery. In the words of Albert Einstein, "There are only two ways to live your life. One is as though nothing is a miracle. The other is as though everything is a miracle."

Every day, I awaken with unbridled joy! My life purpose is now clear. Stress has ebbed from my daily work as I relax into "knowing" how the picture will unfold. I've learned to "be" rather than "do" all the creating I've envisioned. Others join me without my having to search for them; we simply "know" one another when we meet. Now that I have "awakened," the internal alignment I experience acts like a radio frequency, attracting others who are on the same wavelength. "Effort" is a product of the outer world, not the inner world.

attention to the yellow caution lights of life—they're there for a reason!

When I quit my job to start my own business, I didn't have any data that told me I would be successful. The country was preparing to go to war with Iraq, and the economy was in turmoil. Thousands of people were being laid off. I turned down four job offers to follow a dream that meant stepping out on *nothing*—not one client, not one booking, and just a tiny reserve in the bank.

Why did I do it? I *knew* deep down I was doing the right thing. I had unquestionable peace in my soul—a confident assurance that this was the next step I was supposed to take. Today, I always follow my gut instincts, even if I don't have the data to back them up. Following my intuition is one of the core values that I live by.

By now you're probably asking, "So Simon, are you saying I should listen to my intuition for every decision I make?" Yes. Tune in to the decision that brings you peace and act accordingly. Stop and listen to what your heart is telling you on a deep level, and you will know what to do.

Unfortunately, some people are so emotionally disconnected that they don't really know how to tap into their intuition. Until you know what makes you tick and understand how you think and learn, your intuitive intelligence will continue to escape you. You must be in touch with yourself to access your instincts. Get quiet in the moment, listen with your heart, and give up control over the answer. One of the main reasons why people don't trust their intuition is because they don't like what they hear. Their instincts tell them to do something that they don't want to do or are afraid to do, and so they want to believe those instincts are wrong.

People who live their brilliance listen to the wisdom of their intuition. When they follow their intuition, they are at peace, even if they're going against conventional wisdom. Deep inside, a door has opened, and they've seen the light.

Go with your intuition, and let your light brilliantly shine.

PERSONAL APPRAISAL
I invite you to answer the following questions:

1. Do you use your intuition to make the best decisions (small or large) you can?
2. Think about a recent personal or professional decision you've made. What did your intuition tell you to do? How has your decision turned out? Was your intuition correct?
3. Do you believe what your intuition tells you to do? If not, why not? What are you afraid of?

DIAMOND POLISHING
Here are three action steps you can take to polish your facets and ignite your intuition.

1. Do a gut check the next time you're faced with an important decision. Clear your mind. Call a time-out and

go walk around the block. Relax and take a deep breath. Now, get quiet and listen to what your intuition is telling you. If you're still not certain what action to take, sleep on it—literally. Dreams have a way of giving you a preview of "coming attractions." Be open to the message from your dream—it's your intuition talking.

2. Study how to be quiet so that you can access the wisdom of your intuition. Spend fifteen uninterrupted minutes each day simply being quiet. What do you think, hear, sense, and feel? Ask yourself, "How can I live a brilliant life?" Trust me—you will come up with an answer. But you will never get an answer to the question you don't ask.

3. Clean up your workspace. A cluttered desk represents a cluttered mind, and in a cluttered mind, your intuition is like the lost slip of paper that can't make it to the top of the stack. Sometimes you just need to clear your space. The physical act also creates mental order. With an uncluttered mind, hearing your intuition should be effortless and authentic.

A Gem for You
Intuition is peace that surpasses all understanding.

FACET: CHOOSE AUTHENTICITY

"MOST PEOPLE ARE OTHER PEOPLE. THEIR THOUGHTS
ARE SOMEONE ELSE'S OPINIONS, THEIR LIVES
A MIMICRY, THEIR PASSIONS A QUOTATION."

—OSCAR WILDE, BRITISH AUTHOR

Because of their great value and beauty, diamonds are frequently imitated. Some imitations are natural gemstones. Others are synthetic stones, created in a laboratory from substances that resemble diamonds in appearance, such as glass and cubic zirconia (CZ). To the untrained eye, some imitations, like CZ, look very much like a good-quality diamond. Maybe you've heard it said that a good fake is better than the real thing. But don't delude yourself—no imitation diamond will ever be able to replicate the brilliance, the beauty, and the value of an authentic diamond.

The same is true with people. Some people make the choice to live authentic lives every day. These diamond people add value and beauty to the world by releasing the unique brilliance that only they have. Then there are people who look like brilliant diamonds, but on closer inspection are revealed as fake CZs. No matter how hard they try, CZ people cannot open the vault that holds their brilliance because they live in denial about who they truly are.

I used to be a CZ person. When I was first promoted into leadership at the second-largest entertainment company in the world, I felt as if the weight of the world was on my shoulders. Here I was, an African-American man working for a Fortune 50 company in the South. Not only was I representing myself and my family name, but I felt I was representing all African-Americans. I went out of my way to impress my superiors and my staff. To put it simply, I thought that to fit in and be successful, I had to act "white." Even though the company promoted me because I was the right fit for the job, I didn't believe that I was good enough to be in that position. My thoughts, words, and actions were all geared toward trying to be something that I wasn't—a white man trapped in a black man's body. As a result, I led a CZ life with imitation relationships, counterfeit results, and a fake future.

Then one day I came to understand—in the very depths of my soul—that God made me as He wanted me to be. That was the day I took off the mask, accepted myself and my heritage, and decided it was okay to be my authentic self.

You see, God doesn't make CZ. He only makes the real thing: genuine diamonds. We are the ones that get confused. We want to believe that imitation is better than the real thing because it's easier to be an imitation than to be genuine.

Have you ever known someone who appears to have everything, yet is spiritually and emotionally bankrupt? Someone with a PDA full of names and phone numbers, but no meaningful relationships? A person with a full calendar but an empty soul? Others often consider these people very accomplished. But I think of these people as gift wrap—they're so attractive on the outside that you almost forget they're paper thin. They have little depth of character and may never know true success.

A friend of mine once shared a story from high school: The most gorgeous guy in her school, the one every girl wanted to date, had asked her out. But what started out as the best evening of her life quickly turned into the most boring one. The young man was all surface and no soul. On the outside he had lots of sparkle, but underneath, he was nothing but a CZ.

How about you? Are you the real thing? Are you an authentic diamond, or are you a CZ?

Authentic people are comfortable in their own skin. They are true to themselves. They are comfortable being alone and don't have to belong to a particular group to be happy. Genuine diamond people don't see themselves in competition with other diamonds. They understand that no two genuine diamonds are identical, but that each diamond is extraordinary and valuable because it's unique.

A LIVING DIAMOND:
A Real-Life Story from Stuart

As a child, I was overweight and didn't have a lot of friends. Because of this, I spent a great deal of time alone, reading. The things I read inspired me to dream about being thin and accepted. One summer, I read the entire *World Book Encyclopedia*. I read about people, and they became my friends. I dreamed of visiting places and lost myself in these voyages.

I also watched the basketball stars of the day and dreamed of being tall and quick like them. My idol was Wilt Chamberlain, and I watched every game the 76ers played.

One summer, while visiting my relatives in Philadelphia, I was at Fairmont Park when I saw a compact car pull up, and a giant began to get out. It was Wilt Chamberlain!

I ran over to him, and he spoke to me and asked if I liked basketball. Of course, I answered that I loved the game but was too fat to ever be good at it. He told me something I'll always remember: "You are only as good as you think you are. Until you accept yourself and like who you are, you'll never be what you're meant to be."

With that, he passed me the basketball that was in his hands and said, "Let's see your lay-up." I played with him until he left. After that experience, I thought a lot about what he had said.

In time, I became a tall, lanky kid. I chose to play football in high school instead of basketball. I could look over the heads of the defenders and throw a mean spiral. When I graduated from high school, I was six feet, one inch tall and weighed 160 pounds! And, I was voted the student most likely to succeed.

I believe I have succeeded. The two things I always wanted to do were write a book and own a business. Today, I'm an author and the owner of a successful company. I've never forgotten what Wilt Chamberlain said to me that day. Since then, I've visualized myself doing what I dreamed of, and I've accomplished it.

I remember a business lunch I had once with a sixty-nine-year-old gentleman in Southern California. I asked him what life lessons he had to share with me. He said, "Release the need to be absorbed in self. Understand who you are and refrain from always believing you have to impress people." Genuine people don't feel the need to impress others because they recognize their own value and brilliance.

CZ people, however, compare themselves to others, work hard to impress them, and try to make people think they're something they're not. Instead of speaking from the heart and really connecting with others, CZ people are usually busy posturing and being politically correct, especially in business. They will say what is popular and what others want to hear, rather than speaking the truth and dealing with it accordingly.

CZ thinking is the cancer of brilliance. It spreads and affects every aspect of life. CZ people tend to be preoc-

cupied with themselves. For example, they value perfection, so they often have their external "facets" reshaped
and polished with cosmetic surgery. Ironically, they strive
for perfection through imitation. Interestingly, most people think genuine diamonds are perfect, when in fact
they rarely are. Almost all authentic diamonds have inclusions, and yet they shine brilliantly in spite of their
flaws. There is perfection in the imperfection. In other
words, you don't have to be perfect to be brilliant.

CZ thinkers follow the crowd instead of their hearts.
In fact, they need that crowd to reinforce their beliefs.
Authentic people know that when you stand for something, you sometimes stand by yourself. CZ people are
uncomfortable standing alone and often don't stand for
anything at all. They don't want to be the odd person
out, on an island by themselves.

Genuine diamond people are willing to stand alone if
that's what it takes to release their brilliance. Consider
some modern-day examples. Nelson Mandela was im-
prisoned during the prime of his life for standing up
against apartheid in his homeland of South Africa. When
he was finally released after twenty-seven years, instead
of seeking vengeance, he forgave his captors and those
who had wreaked havoc on black South Africans. His
love for humanity has forever changed his country—and
many would say, the world—for the better.

Erin Brockovich, a single mother of three with no
legal background, uncovered evidence of a potentially
lethal contamination in the groundwater in Hinkley,

California, by Pacific Gas & Electric. Fighting against a huge company, the legal system, and occasionally the town she was trying to help, Brockovich and a team of lawyers eventually won the biggest settlement on record, $333 million, for a civil class-action lawsuit.

When you decide to step out of the pack and be your authentic self, your friends and co-workers may look at you differently. But genuine people are comfortable saying, "I'm okay with me even if you're not okay with me." They act on their convictions without fearing what other people might say or do.

Am I telling you to be a loner? No, of course not. But I am telling you that if you desire to live an authentic, brilliant life, there may be times when you have to walk alone. And yet, at the same time, I believe there are people just waiting in the wings for someone to step out of the crowd and be boldly different. When you choose to be the genuine diamond God meant for you to be, you will attract like-minded passionate, brilliant people who will stand with you.

Today, I invite you to look in the mirror, take off the mask, and strip away all that's preventing the real you from shining through. Recognize who you genuinely are, and choose to live an authentic life in which you brilliantly shine from the inside out. Realize that authentic living is a process and that it takes time. An imitation, a manufactured person will never have the same depth, strength, or resilience as a genuine person who has been refined by fire.

Imagine what the world would be like if everyone authentically loved who they were and didn't feel compelled to conform to society's perceptions of success, wealth, and beauty.

PERSONAL APPRAISAL
I invite you to answer the following questions:

1. Can you identify times in your life when you operated in total authenticity? What did it feel like? How does that feeling compare to those times when you operated with a CZ mentality? Going forward, which way do you prefer to live?
2. Are you afraid to speak your truth? When was the last time you stepped out of the crowd and took bold action, or made a bold suggestion or statement, that ruffled the feathers of the establishment?
3. How will you model authenticity for those who look to you as a mentor?

DIAMOND POLISHING
Here are three action steps you can take to polish your facets and choose authenticity.

1. Ask your spouse, significant other, Accountability Partner, or friend if he or she perceives that you spend most of your life living authentically or as a CZ. Then, ask that person for specific suggestions on how you can choose authenticity more often.

2. Make the commitment to rid yourself of CZ language, thinking, and beliefs that dim your brilliance.

3. Consider the decisions you have to make this week that may force you to be ostracized from the clique, the club, your friends, or your co-workers. Is it worth it to choose authenticity?

♦ Visit www.ReleasingBrilliance.com for more resources, exercises, tips, and tools for living authentically.

A GEM FOR YOU
Are you an authentic diamond, or are you a CZ?

CUT: TAKE BOLD ACTION

"IT IS EASY TO SIT UP AND TAKE NOTICE. WHAT IS DIFFICULT IS GETTING UP AND TAKING ACTION."

—AL BATT, HUMORIST

A good cut is essential to reveal a diamond's true beauty and brilliance. Without it, even a diamond with outstanding clarity and color won't display the sparkle for which diamonds are famous. Cut (not to be confused with a diamond's shape, such as round, square, oval, or pear) refers to the facets a skilled craftsman creates in transforming a piece of rough diamond into a polished one. The better the cut, the more valuable the diamond. A diamond cut to perfect proportions achieves maximum brilliance. It internally reflects light from one mirror-like facet to another and then out through the top of the stone. Diamonds that are cut either too deep or too shallow lose light through the sides or bottom, resulting in dull, dark, lifeless stones.

A diamond can't reveal its brilliance until a master cutter takes action. Likewise, you won't discover and reveal your brilliance until you take specific action. To release your brilliance, you must polish the facets of relationships, fears, habits, language, and influence. As you take action on each of these facets, the resulting experiences will shape you and smooth your rough edges. Once a diamond is cut, it's one of the strongest substances on Earth. When you take action, the associated thoughts, feelings, and confidence become imbedded in the core of your being. Action makes you stronger.

A diamond can take any number of shapes, and so can your diamond brilliance. It doesn't matter what form it takes. The important thing is that the diamond has been transformed through a series of choices and actions. Every rough piece has the potential to be a priceless gem. Similarly, every one of us has the potential to achieve greatness and make a priceless contribution. It's all in the cut.

♦ Visit www.ReleasingBrilliance.com for more resources, exercises, tips, and tools for action planning.

A GEM FOR YOU
Action makes you stronger.

FACET: INVEST IN RELATIONSHIP CAPITAL

Not too long ago, I hosted a dinner party for a few friends, and the evening transitioned into an informal discussion group in which we talked about everything under the sun. In three hours we covered politics, spirituality, movies, business, wealth, race, and relationships. The dialogue was effortless, and the conversation priceless. It was refreshing to see a group of individuals be so transparent and authentic. Needless to say, we solved all of the world's problems in just one evening!

One of the most popular discussion questions was "How can we maintain healthy relationships?" One person said that mutual values that are non-negotiable when the going gets tough are essential. Another said the secret is to respect, appreciate, and celebrate the other person by being his or her biggest fan.

The conversation got me thinking, and after our guests left, I turned to my wife and asked, "Who, really, are our friends?" Every year we exchange holiday cards with many individuals and couples, and yet we could count on two hands the relationships that were meaningful to us. That insight was an epiphany for us, and we committed to focusing on and investing in our most significant relationships.

What is a meaningful relationship? I believe, first and foremost, it is one in which both people are authentic. Meaningful relationships strengthen your emotional alignment by inviting you to remove your mask and let down the façade that prevents you from being authentic. You can be yourself, speak your mind, and fall flat on your face, and the other person will still love you for who you are. These connections are based on implicit trust. There is no need to play mind games, and you never have to question the other person's motives.

Genuine relationships have depth because they are based on shared values that strengthen the bond over time. In a meaningful relationship, each of you desires to contribute to the relationship and to the other person's life. Authentic friends are those you can call at 3:00 A.M. to help you, and you know they will . . . joyfully.

In contrast, performance-driven relationships are forged out of convenience and selfishness. Simply put, these relationships are not about who you are; they're about what you do. Your approval of each other is based on how well you have performed, as in "What have you done for me lately?" These relationships tend to be superficial, with no real depth. People who have mostly performance-driven relationships often find themselves lonely.

Let me give you an example of each kind of relationship. I have two great friends, Calvin and Louis, with whom I have meaningful relationships. Although they live in different cities, we talk at least once a week. They are my Accountability Partners, and they continually challenge me to stretch beyond my current abilities. They know they can depend on me, and I on them. No one keeps track of the relationship debits and credits; we just flow.

In the past, my wife Renee and I had several performance-driven relationships, but we chose to step away from them. In each case, the relationship was out of balance—it was all about the other people and rarely about us. We were chips in their game. When we chose not to meet their demands or play their games according to their rules, it became clear that these people were not authentic friends, so we ended the relationships. Life is simply too short to invest in a losing proposition.

How can you tell whether a relationship is meaningful or performance driven? First, check your heart—your intuition will give you a clue. Then, consider whether the relationship encourages you to stay in emotional alignment or causes you to be pulled out of alignment. In authentic relationships, you don't have to worry about what others think about you or where you stand. Your fulfillment comes from within you as you add value to another person's life. By comparison, in performance-driven relationships, your fulfillment comes from external sources. You constantly feel the need to please others and to know where you stand with them.

Author and speaker George Frazier advises us to carefully choose the people we associate with because everyone in our life does one of four things: adds to us, subtracts from us, multiplies us, or divides us. Under his theory, meaningful relationships are those with people who add to you or multiply you, and performance-driven relationships are those with people who subtract from you or divide you. Authentic relationships polish and shape you so you can shine even more brilliantly, while performance-driven relationships diminish your brilliance.

Who are your friends? Why are they your friends? Are they genuine friends, or are they truly just acquaintances? Do they add to, subtract from, multiply, or divide you?

Remember that you will become like the people you associate with the most. You grow in the context of your relationships. If your relationships have limited content, then your context will be limited. Whoever speaks into your ear speaks into your life.

A LIVING DIAMOND:
A Real-Life Story from Lawrence

Your environment and the people with whom you choose to associate are critical to your success.

Several years ago, I found myself in Des Moines, Iowa, driving around the snow-covered streets with a car full of "crackheads," when I looked in my rearview mirror and saw a police car. I panicked and yelled, "Everyone put your dope and pipes away! There's a cop behind us!"

I just knew the police officer would pull me over and find a car full of drugs. I had enough cocaine, in fact, that had I been caught, I'd be in prison today instead of being clean and sober for the past seventeen years.

It was a blessing I wasn't pulled over, and today, I can tell a different story.

Now, I choose to surround myself with other doers—people with purpose—and my reality has changed. I am living my dream. I'm now the father and husband I always wanted to be. My children are exceptional students and athletes, and my wife is the love of my life. We travel as a family to exotic places around the world. I've become a "millionaire maker," and I have the opportunity to make a positive impact on the lives of countless others.

With that in mind, I invite you to evaluate your relationship wealth. Are you friend rich, but relationship poor? I suggest you analyze your relationships just as you would your stock portfolio. If you have stocks or mutual funds that are consistently doing well and increasing your wealth, what do you do? You probably invest more money in them. Conversely, if you have stocks that continually underperform and drain your wealth, do you keep them? No, of course not. You sell them and invest your money in something that will give you a better return on your investment.

Now analyze your "Relationship Portfolio" the same way. Identify which people and relationships reduce your self-worth and dim your brilliance, and phase them out of your life. Then, invest more time and energy in those people and relationships that increase and expand your brilliance. If you grow your Relationship Portfolio with connections that add to you and multiply you, over time you will become a relationship millionaire.

Investing in relationship capital is a lot like investing in the stock market. Both should be considered long-term investments. If you want to grow your money, you invest in growth stocks. If you're serious about personal growth, you should invest heavily in "growth" relationships. Work to establish and maintain authentic relationships with people who are several steps ahead of you in the Crown Facets you most want to work on and who will stretch you, push you, and encourage you to be better than you've ever been before. And remember, if a relationship reduces you in any way, then you're no longer making a return on that relationship, and it's time to "sell off." Stop investing your time, energy, emotions, and intellect in something—and someone—that diminishes who you are.

I recommend diversifying your Relationship Portfolio by investing heavily in three different growth relationships, each in a different core area of your life (for example, financial, spiritual, and professional). If you focus on more than three, you can't devote enough time or energy to get a return on your investment. These relationships offer mentoring, expand your worldview, and accelerate your learning. Just one of these relationships can make a tremendous difference in how your life turns out.

Of all the relationships in your portfolio, if you're married, the one with your spouse is far and away the most important. It deserves your utmost attention because it's the relationship that can bring the most value to your life. Your spouse, more than anyone else, should add to you and multiply you. Furthermore, *your spouse provides a critical part of the combination to the vault where your brilliance is kept. He or she can polish you and help you reveal your brilliance like no one else.*

If you have only enough time and energy to invest in one relationship, this should be it. Check in regularly and often with your spouse—not on a superficial level, but on a deep emotional level. As with your investments, if you ignore your relationship with your spouse, over time it will lose its value. Then you become out of sync, disconnected from your soul mate. Marriage works only if you invest yourself in it.

EXERCISE: *Grow Your Relationship Portfolio*

1. Choose three core areas of your life (*spiritual, family, career, emotional, mental, wellness, social, financial*) in which you'd like to improve.

2. For each core area, identify the individual(s) with whom you'd like to build or enhance a relationship in order to grow and stretch yourself.

3. Identify how, specifically, you will invest in each relationship.

Core Area	Relationship	How I Will Invest in This Relationship

Invest in meaningful relationship capital, and you will increase your self-worth and your relationship wealth. If you have lots of acquaintances but few genuine relationships, you are friend rich but relationship poor. Quality relationships provide the environment for one diamond to polish another and for both to release their brilliance.

PERSONAL APPRAISAL

I invite you to answer the following questions:

1. Which of your relationships are authentic and meaningful, and which are performance driven?
2. Do you add to, subtract from, multiply, or divide the people in your life? Do you expand or drain other people's lives?
3. What can you do to increase your relationship capital? How can you invest more in the significant relationships in your life? Do you consistently look for ways to strengthen your relationships with those you care about?

DIAMOND POLISHING

Here are three action steps you can take to polish your facets and invest in relationship capital.

1. Identify three ways you can invest more in your relationship with your spouse.
2. Build relationship capital with others by finding out what is important to them. Ask them how you can help them

fulfill their Universal Assignment. Discover what they need from you within the context of your relationship.

3. Leverage your brilliance in authentic relationships so that both you and the other person will benefit.

♦ Visit www.ReleasingBrilliance.com for more resources, exercises, tips, and tools for building your Relationship Portfolio.

A GEM FOR YOU
Are you friend rich but relationship poor?

FACET: AWAKEN THE LION WITHIN YOU

Gordon Dalby, an author and a graduate of Duke, Stanford, and Harvard universities, tells a story about a man who had a terrifying recurrent dream. In the man's nightmare, a ferocious lion kept chasing him until he dropped, exhausted, and awoke screaming.

Eventually, the man told a friend about his frightening dreams. Assuming the lion represented something fearful in the man's life, the friend suggested that perhaps it symbolized his boss or wife. Then the friend gave the man some advice: The next time he had the dream, he should try to not run away from the lion. Instead, he should stand firm and ask the lion who or what he was and what he was doing in the man's life.

Before long, the man had the dream again. He watched in fear as the lion approached, shaking its massive head and baring its dagger-like teeth. Trembling, the man asked, "Who are you? What do you want?" The lion replied, "I am your courage and your strength! Why do you keep running away from me?"

I so appreciate simple stories like this one that just hit you between the eyes with their truth and wisdom! Isn't it so true that often the things we fear the most turn out to be nothing at all? We all have courage, but like our brilliance, we don't always recognize it for what it is.

Fear is powerful. Only love is equal to it in emotional intensity. But whereas love typically moves us to action, fear tends to stop us in our tracks. Fear keeps us from doing the things we know we should do and prevents us from moving toward our hearts' desires. You've probably heard the acronym for FEAR: False Evidence Appearing Real. Our fears create filters that distort the truth and alter our view of reality. Fear filters choke our courage and squelch our hope. Consequently, we simply sit back and do nothing, or even worse, we crawl back in our shells like turtles and hide.

It seems the list of things we fear is almost endless. Naturally, many people fear illness, disease, and death. We fear criminals, natural disasters, and poverty. And then we each have our own phobias. On top of all that, we fear being rejected, being different . . . and being the same. We're afraid of being laughed at and of what people might think of us. We're afraid we won't live up to others' expectations . . . or our own. We're afraid of failure, and we're afraid of success. Yes, that's right: All too often, we fear success. We're afraid of the sheer

power of our brilliance, our light, and of being the dazzling diamond we were meant to be.

What do you fear? What are you running away from?

When my father immigrated to the United States from
Jamaica some forty years ago, he wanted his slice of the
American pie. But he was afraid that his accent, his lack
of education, and his skin color would hold him back.
He focused on what he didn't have and why he might fail
instead of why he could succeed. Eventually, he realized
he had no choice but to make something of his life in
America. There was nothing for him to return to in Jamaica. With sheer determination, he rose above his fears
and went on to live a fulfilling life. Nevertheless, I wonder how many years he spent giving in to his fears.

It's easy to fall into the trap of blaming someone or
something for your lack of success. Until you become
personally accountable for your life—for how you
think, what you believe, and how you act—you won't
be able to defeat your fears. So stop playing the victim,
summon the courageous lion within you, and get on
with your life.

Fear can be your friend instead of your foe if you
learn to use it to your advantage. Overcoming that
which you fear is one key that will unlock the vault
where your brilliance is hidden. Conquering your
fears releases the genius within you and allows your
light to shine.

The courage you need to defeat your fears can take
many forms. Often, you can take small steps to overcome

your fears. A good example is public speaking. Each small step gives you the confidence and strength to take the next step, and the next one, and the next. Courage is a habit that you need to develop every day. Author Mary Anne Radmacher tells us, "Courage doesn't always roar. Sometimes courage is the little voice at the end of the day that says, 'I'll try again tomorrow.'" Over time, bit by bit, you'll make progress. Then one day you'll look up and realize you've triumphed over your fear.

Other times, your fear will be a type that must be overcome in one fell swoop. When you fear something like flying on an airplane, you have to jump in feet first and face your fear head on. In these cases, courage is a decision to take immediate and profound action. Once you recover from the sheer terror, you experience the absolute euphoria of defeating your fear. At that moment, you know you can—and will—rise above all your fears.

It takes courage to stand up for what you believe in, especially if you have to stand by yourself. Throughout history we've seen many great examples of courage, such as Martin Luther King Jr., Mahatma Gandhi, and Mother Teresa, but the world always needs more courageous people. What about you? You don't have to take on the whole world to show your courage. Start with your own world. What can you do in your community, in your school, in your organization, in your family, in your life?

Here's an interesting tidbit of information: In the Middle Ages, rings set with precious stones were considered not so much pieces of jewelry, but rather amulets that conveyed magical powers on the wearer, such as fearlessness and invincibility. Monarchs began wearing diamonds as symbols of power and courage. Likewise, your diamond brilliance can be a symbol, a model of fearlessness and courage to those around you. You are no less a diamond than the great leaders of history. You simply haven't developed as much courage—*yet*.

In the words of motivational speaker Michael Pritchard, "Fear is that little darkroom where negatives are developed." The more we dwell on our fears, the more negative we become—about ourselves, our lives, our futures.

Where is your digital camera? Snap a picture of your future! Do you have the guts to pursue something you've never had before in order to become something you've never been before? Step out of the darkroom of self-limiting fears, step into the future you were meant to have, and be a beautiful, brilliant, and bold picture of courage.

PERSONAL APPRAISAL
I invite you to answer the following questions:

1. What are your three greatest fears?
2. What could you be, do, or have in your life if you overcame these three fears?
3. If you knew you would make a difference, would you have the courage to step out, take a risk, and stand up for what you believe in?

A LIVING DIAMOND:
A Real-Life Story from Cooper

For as long as I can remember, I've wanted to fly jet airplanes. As a kid, I built every model airplane I could get my hands on and then hung them from the ceiling in my room. I spent hours at the local airport, dreaming of what it would be like to be a pilot. But growing up, I was never encouraged to follow my dream because "successful" people didn't fly airplanes for a living. "Successful" people were in business. By the time I went to college, the dream had faded.

There's a proverb that says, "One's best fortune, or their worst, is their spouse." My wife is undoubtedly my best fortune in so many ways. My dream of becoming a pilot was rekindled when she gave me flying lessons for a wedding gift. It was then that I found my brilliance—a natural talent for flying. It comes so easily for me. When I fly, I'm energized, engaged, in the flow.

I began to think again about flying as a career. But there were so many uncertainties: How would we make ends meet on a pilot's salary? (Contrary to popular belief, salaries for entry-level pilots are barely above poverty level.) Could our marriage survive a pilot's schedule? Could I travel that much and still be the kind of father I wanted to be? My fears kept me from moving forward.

Eventually, I reached a point where I couldn't bear the thought of sitting at a desk for the next thirty years when I knew I had what it took to be a pilot. My marriage and family were now strong enough to survive a pilot's lifestyle, and my wife and kids became my biggest cheerleaders. For the next two years, I worked my "day job" to earn a living, and left my family every weekend to fly skydivers in a town ninety miles away. I spent my Saturday nights sleeping on an air mattress in a hangar at the airport. By September of 2001, I had the qualifications to get a job with a regional airline. And then came 9-11.

Clearly, the effects of 9-11 on my life were nothing compared to what thousands of others experienced. The disaster shook the airline industry to its core and ended or stymied the careers of thousands of pilots. To be so close to achieving a lifelong dream I'd worked so hard for and then have it taken away—possibly forever—was a devastating blow. There were so many times when I wanted to quit, but my wife wouldn't let me. She always asked what kind of message that would send to our children. So, I'd take a step back, look for another path, and try again. I chose to take action, to keep moving forward.

Finally, three years later, the job offers started coming. To date, all five offers have been in the $20,000 salary range, based out of other cities, and involved challenging schedules (including being on call 24-7). Even so, let me tell you, it took courage and faith to turn down those offers. Why did I turn them down? Because they weren't right for my family. You don't live your brilliance in a vacuum. How you use your gifts and talents affects the other people in your life.

I believe eventually a flying job will come that will better balance my dream with my family's needs. When it does, as exciting as it will be, I know it will take courage to walk away from a good salary and a known lifestyle and step into the unknown. I still have many of the same fears about how everything will work out, but now I don't allow my fears to stop me. My motto is "I'll cross that bridge when I come to it."

Living a brilliant life doesn't necessarily come easily. If you look too far into the future, you might think you'll never get there. Just keep taking that next step and celebrate the small achievements along the way. And remember, living your brilliance is a marathon, not a sprint.

DIAMOND POLISHING

Here are three action steps you can take to polish your facets and awaken the courageous lion within you.

1. Think about fears you've had in the past and how you overcame them. Write down the lessons you learned from those experiences that you can use to eliminate current and future fears.
2. In your quiet time (such as fifteen minutes before starting your day), minimize your fears and maximize the exact opposite: your desired outcomes. Imagine what it would be like to overcome these fears.

3. Think about and write down what fears you would have to overcome in order to live an authentic life. Then develop and write down how you plan to conquer those fears.

A Gem for You
We are afraid of the sheer power of our brilliance, of being the dazzling diamonds we were meant to be.

FACET: UPGRADE YOUR VERBAL SOFTWARE

"MAN ACTS AS THOUGH HE WERE THE SHAPER AND
MASTER OF LANGUAGE, WHILE IN FACT LANGUAGE
REMAINS THE MASTER OF MAN."

–MARTIN HEIDEGGER, GERMAN PHILOSOPHER

According to *The Cambridge Encyclopedia of the English Language*, there are more than one million words in the English language. But we only use between two thousand and twenty-five hundred words, just a small proportion of the many available to us. And, according to the Robbins Research Institute, each of us has only two hundred to three hundred habitual words that we use regularly to frame our reality.

Language is the software of the mind. Like software, language is simply a tool that we use to create a specific outcome. Words paint pictures. Words express thoughts and communicate emotions.

Brilliant words motivate people to act, and lifeless words cause people to disengage and settle for mediocrity.

Let me invite you to upgrade your verbal software so that you can access your desired outcomes faster—at broadband speeds rather than at dial-up speeds. How? By using Life Language—powerful words that capture the very essence of life itself. Life Language ignites the spirit and engages the heart to reach for the stars. It empowers those who feel powerless. There's a proverb that says, "Death and life is in the power of the tongue." Brilliant people speak in life-enhancing terms.

Here are some examples of life-draining language versus life-enhancing language.

Life-draining phrases	Life-enhancing phrases
I'm just dying to know.	I would love to know.
It's killing me.	I will overcome this.
I don't know if I'm good enough.	I'm the best person for this opportunity.
I never have enough to make ends meet.	I am surrounded by abundance and have more than enough.
I am so lost in life.	I'm moving forward with my life.

People who live their brilliance have one thing in common: They empower themselves by skillfully using Life Language to change themselves and ultimately change how they view the world around them.

Your life right now is the sum total of every word you've ever spoken—in your head and out loud. Twentieth-century philosopher Ludwig Josef Johann Wittgenstein is quoted as saying, "The limits of my language mean the limits of my world." The words you use determine your beliefs. Your beliefs lead to decisions. Your decisions produce results—some good, some bad. It all depends on your language.

How do I know? For many years, I had very low self-esteem. I was broke, both spiritually and financially. I believed that all of the cushy assignments, growth opportunities, and great perks went to the popular people. I didn't even have the opportunity to compete on a level playing field because I believed the deck was stacked against me—I came from the wrong side of the tracks, and I didn't have a blue-blood pedigree or an Ivy League education. What I brought to the table wasn't accepted, so why should I continue to try? In my mind, I was constantly telling myself that everyone else was better than I was. That thought became a belief, and that belief became my reality. My internal language sabotaged my success. I was afraid to accept responsibility for my success, because if I failed, I would have no one to blame but myself.

One day, after I had thrown myself a huge pity party, someone invited me to a seminar that would prove to be a turning point in my life. The speaker that day was Dr. Mike Murdock, founder of The Wisdom Center. Dr. Murdock spoke about some profound truths, and a light went on in my head. I came to accept that I was the one with the problem, not other people. And I realized that as long as I continued to talk about my shortfalls and impoverished mentality, I would continue to attract more of the same.

Dr. Murdock encouraged everyone to go home and write a sixty-second "commercial" or affirmation and begin to internalize it. Here is the commercial I wrote.

I am stepping into greatness! I am a unique, new kind of person the world has never before seen and will never see the likes of again. I was born to do great things.

I have always been special. When I came into the world, there was a mark of greatness stamped upon my life. The kiss of God is upon my life.

I was born to be a blessing to millions of people around the world. I was born to succeed as a husband, father, speaker, author, business leader, investor, and life coach.

I am energetic.

I am alive and happy.

My spirit is contagious.

I am authentic.

I am in touch with my feelings.

I am anointed.

I am intelligent.

I am a creative genius.

I am in demand as a professional speaker.

I am a child of God.

I am a leader.

I am a big thinker.
I am financially independent.
I am Chairman of the Board.
I am a man of great faith.
I am wealthy internally and externally.
I am attractive.
I am a hard worker.
I am a finisher.
And as gifted as I am, I should know that all of
Heaven is waiting to help me make every dream a
reality! Everything is possible if I believe. I was
born to taste the grapes, so I will reach for the wine
of life as I embrace this moment!

In the years since I wrote that, my life has changed dramatically. You can make dramatic changes in your life, too. If you want to change your future, then inspect your present. If you want to change the results you're getting, then change your language. Upgrade your verbal software and begin to speak the language of the life you want instead of the life you want to leave behind. Cancel out your negative statements and thoughts with absolutely positive ones, and watch what happens.

You are the prophet of your future. Every word you release into the universe has the creative energy and potential to manifest your future. Powerful, life-enhancing words are the catalysts for launching new ideas, uplifting your spirit, and releasing your brilliance.

PERSONAL APPRAISAL

I invite you to answer the following questions:

1. What are the habitual words that you use on a daily basis?
2. Is your language moving you away from or toward your desired outcomes?
3. Is there any dysfunctional language in your history that is sabotaging your future?

A LIVING DIAMOND:
A Real-Life Story from Anita

Until I was thirteen, I flourished. I was a happy, content child who soared in school, in friendships, and most importantly, in self-confidence. Then I was sexually abused.

The trauma inflicted by sexual abuse is so deeply painful it diminishes one's spirit. Without a doubt, my ability to believe in myself was lost due to the acts of two selfish men. I blamed myself for "causing" the abuse. I began to slouch on purpose to hide my breasts. I lost all my confidence. I felt worthless. I struggle to this day to believe in myself.

Despite this cruel interruption in my development, I managed to go on. I was one of the "lucky" few, primarily because I had some protective factors in my home and school environments. Namely, I had a mother who believed in me and had high expectations for me.

At times, my mother, who had repressed memories of being repeatedly sexually abused most of her childhood, could be verbally abusive and overbearing. Looking back, I realize now that she was hurting too, but she didn't know why. We are never taught how to be a parent—the most important job we can ever have—so I know my mom did the best she could given the ghosts from her childhood. She never meant to douse my spirit. This verbally abusive dimension was manifested as a response to stress, plain and simple. Nevertheless, I didn't understand those dynamics when I was young, so it hurt and added to my self-doubt.

We are products of our childhood. Every day, I let my daughter know how very much I love her and that I believe in her. I pray to God that no one ever crushes her spirit. She is full of life and knows nothing of the ugliness I've had to overcome. My daughter, like every child, deserves to always remain self-assured and confident. She has so much potential. As a parent, I use the power of encouraging words and love to guide her.

People are always surprised when they learn I'm a survivor of child abuse. Apparently, I don't look the part. I come from a hard-working, close-knit, upper middle-class family. I was a model. I achieved a higher education, and I am an accomplished health-care executive.

So, how did I successfully emerge from this challenging experience? Through encouragement and support from key people in my life who believe in me. My mother loved me and took every opportunity to tell me that each day. The power of words has been instrumental in rebuilding my self-esteem. Four simple words make such a big difference: *I believe in you.* What transformed me from an insecure, shaking adult was people believing in me—and me learning to once again believe in myself. I realized that my wonderful husband, talented daughter, friends, bosses, family members—all people I admire—couldn't be wrong.

Part of my brilliance is that I'm persistent and determined. I had goals, and I never gave up on my dreams or myself. I recited daily affirmations. I took on challenges that were scary and overwhelming. I learned it really is true that you can do anything you put your mind to.

I have more than succeeded! I rediscovered my potential and ultimately, most importantly, my belief in myself.

DIAMOND POLISHING

Here are three action steps you can take to polish your facets and upgrade your verbal software.

1. Identify your top ten favorite words that describe the person you are becoming.
2. Think about disempowering words or phrases that were said to you when you were growing up. Write them down. Then, write down the most powerfully positive, life-enhancing phrase you can think of to replace each one. For example, replace "You're a sore loser" with "I'm an awesome winner."

3. Write your own personal commercial or affirmation. Use the space below to draft a three- to five-sentence message that will remind you of your brilliance. For help in this important endeavor, pick up a copy of *Stand Up for Your Life* by Cheryl Richardson. It will provide you with new, self-honoring strategies to help you realize your greatest potential.

_____

_____

_____

_____

_____

_____

_____

_____

_____

_____

_____

_____

_____

_____

_____

_____

_____

_____

_____

A Gem for You

You are the prophet of your future. Use Life Language to create your brilliant future.

FACET: DEVELOP HIGH-IMPACT HABITS

"HABIT, MY FRIEND, IS PRACTICE LONG PURSUED,
THAT AT LAST BECOMES MAN HIMSELF."

–EVENUS, ANCIENT GREEK POET

People often ask me how I was able to establish such a thriving business less than two years after leaving my job. Well, today I'm going to reveal one of my secrets.

Remember the Mike Murdock seminar I told you about in the last chapter? Well, here is another piece of wisdom from Dr. Murdock. He said, "You do not decide your future. You decide your habits, and your habits decide your future!" He then went on to say, "The secret of your future is hidden in your daily routine."

I was struck by the simplistic nature of those statements. And I decided to find out if what he said was true.

I started to affirm myself every day by reading aloud the commercial I shared with you in the last chapter. It has become a daily habit for me. Rehearsing my commercial was awkward at first, but then I really started to believe what I was saying. I have reprogrammed my mind and my spirit by releasing into the universe the words that are full of my energy and are congruent with my internal truth. When you convince *yourself* you can succeed, there's no way you can't!

Replaying my commercial every day was the kick-start I needed to change my life. Then I rolled up my sleeves and went to work. I began rising early every morning to spend fifteen minutes writing my business plan, creating a client target list, or writing a chapter for my first book. In the old days, I got up just in time to shower, shave, and get to work. But I decided to develop the habit of getting up early, and soon fifteen minutes turned into three hours. My entire being became consumed with making my dream a reality.

So what's the point? When I was seventeen years old, I started saying I wanted to speak all over the world. However, saying something is one thing; actually *doing* it is something completely different. It wasn't until fifteen years later, at age thirty-two, that I began to *act* on what I'd been saying all those years. Affirmations plus action were the key for me. Believe it or not, it worked. I know from first-hand experience that what Mike Murdock said is true: Your future *does* lie in your present-day habits and daily routine.

Humans become conditioned to behave a certain way by repetition. To change a particular behavior, you have to reprogram or rewire the brain by repeating a new, different behavior over and over and over again until new synapses are created. Eventually, if the new behavior is repeated often enough and long enough, you begin to see results. Although it's been said that it takes only thirty days of repeated behavior to develop a habit, research indicates that it actually takes at least three to six months to create a solid one. You will know you've successfully developed new behaviors when other people start noticing the change in you.

One of the most crucial things you can do to improve your life is to develop *high-impact habits*. These are the behaviors and actions that will move you farthest and fastest in the direction of your heart's desire. High-impact activities accelerate the process of opening the vault and releasing your brilliance. Low-impact activities, however, drain your energy, your enthusiasm, and your efforts and prevent you from maximizing your brilliance.

What is the number-one high-impact habit? Rehearsing your commercial every day, without fail, starting now. Repeat it at least twice a day—once in the morning and once in the evening—and anytime you think about it, such as when you're sitting in traffic. Declare it out loud, and it will begin to reverberate and vibrate within your internal being.

Develop a habit of being a steward of your time and energy. What you do with these two resources will determine the outcome of your life. Time is the most precious asset on the planet, and yet we tend to let it slip away on activities that don't move us forward. How much time do you spend watching TV, answering e-mail, and surfing the Internet? I'll be the first to admit that I waste far too much time on those three things alone. I remind myself daily that if I'm going to reach my financial and life goals, I can't let these low-impact activities consume my day.

To help get control of the time I spend on e-mail, I developed a new habit that I recommend you try too: I restrict myself to checking e-mail only twice a day. Give it a try. Create two time blocks—one in the morning and one in the afternoon—to answer all your messages. You'll be astounded at the amount of time you'll free up for the crucial high-impact activities. And to stop wasting hours absorbed in the Internet, I made a new rule for myself: I surf the net only with a specific purpose in mind.

How about you? What low-impact habits do you need to break? Can you limit the amount of time you spend watching TV, or reading the sports page, or playing computer games, so that you can focus on developing a skill set that will move you closer to your dreams and goals?

EXERCISE: *Developing High-Impact Habits*

For each of the eight Crown Facets of your life, identify and write down:
- One low-impact habit that you should stop doing
- One high-impact habit that you should start doing
- One brilliant habit that you already have and should continue

CROWN FACET	HIGH-IMPACT HABITS		
	STOP *Low-Impact Habits*	START *High-Impact Habits*	CONTINUE *Brilliant Habits*
Spiritual			
Family			
Career			
Emotional			
Mental			
Wellness			
Social			
Financial			

One of the best habits I developed grew out of those extra fifteen minutes I found each morning, and it has literally transformed my life. I suggest you give it a try: Create a habit of guarding your energy and protecting your spirit with your own personal Hour of Power every morning—twenty minutes of meditation, twenty minutes of exercise, and twenty minutes of reading out loud.

Meditating focuses your energy and intention on how your brilliant day will unfold. Exercising invigorates your body and creates energy and momentum for your entire day. Reading focuses your mind. We live in an electronic world that moves at the speed of light. We have instant access to virtually any kind of information. Unfortunately, that has created in us an attention deficit, and we've forgotten how to focus our minds. Reading out loud not only keeps you focused, but also expands your vocabulary, increases your confidence, and allows you to interact with the author's message.

Aristotle said, "It is well to be up before daybreak, for such habits contribute to health, wealth, and wisdom." When you focus on the high-impact activities in your life and commit to making each of them a habit, your brilliance will shine like never before.

PERSONAL APPRAISAL

I invite you to answer the following questions:

1. What are your top three priorities—the three activities that will have the most significant, most positive impact on your quest to release and live your brilliance?
2. Have you made these priorities part of your daily routine? Are they habits?
3. What new high-impact habit can you begin today?

A LIVING DIAMOND:
A Real-Life Story from Beatrice

I've made it a habit to remember people's names. This may seem like just a social skill, but it really makes a good impression in your professional life when you can use a person's name at a second or third meeting without asking for a reintroduction.

In college, I was president of an honor society, and each semester we inducted about eighty people. I would see their names over and over again. By the time I met them, I knew all their names. I also paid attention to conversations to see who was who. Usually, by the second meeting, I knew the faces that went with the names.

I specifically remember one initiates' meeting where I had to write names on a chalkboard under different volunteer projects. When people raised their hands to volunteer, I acknowledged them with, "Thank you . . ." and then their first names. The room was filled with whispers about how I was able to do that.

Today, in my career, success has a lot to do with whom you know. When I call someone by name, it allows me the pleasure of that person's attention and perhaps some conversation. In some ways, it shows I'm astute and intelligent.

Greeting people by name equates to hugging them. It's a welcoming sign on your part and shows that they're special enough for you to remember their name. It helps me make friends quickly. I'm glad to give this warmth to those I meet. I find I'm usually greeted with a smile in return.

DIAMOND POLISHING

Here are three action steps you can take to polish your facets and develop high-impact habits.

1. For the next seven days, keep a list of your daily activities. Determine which activities are high impact—yielding the highest results and brilliance—and which ones are low impact, yielding low results. After seven days, ask yourself, "Which activities help me release my brilliance and make me more effective?"
2. Begin every day by embracing and practicing the Hour of Power techniques to sharpen your focus for the day.
3. Review each of the fifteen facets in this book and determine which is the most important one—the one on

which you need to get clarity immediately. Share this information with your Accountability Partner and ask him or her to hold you accountable for developing a new habit for that facet. Then carve out fifteen minutes in the morning or evening and take action that will begin your new habit. Repeat this every day until you no longer have to remind yourself to do it.

A GEM FOR YOU

High-impact habits accelerate the process of opening the vault and releasing your brilliance.

FACET: CHANGE YOUR WORLD

"WHEN YOU EMPOWER PEOPLE, YOU'RE NOT
INFLUENCING JUST THEM; YOU'RE INFLUENCING ALL
THE PEOPLE THEY INFLUENCE."

–JOHN MAXWELL, AUTHOR

Ludwig van Beethoven's Fifth Symphony is one of the most memorable and influential compositions in classical music. According to journalist Peter Gutmann, Beethoven struggled for more than a decade to develop the full potential of the symphony, constantly simplifying and tightening the work. His influence ultimately ushered in an important period in music known as the Romantic era in the early 1800s. Unable to conceive of the enormous impact he would have, Beethoven suffered from severe inner turmoil and a constant feeling of insignificance. But his artistic vision was irrepressible.

Though he began going deaf as a young man, and indeed was completely deaf in the last several years of his life, Beethoven's disability did not hinder his brilliance as a composer. In fact, most of his great compositions, including the stirring Fifth Symphony, were composed after he began losing his hearing. Beethoven's influence on the world is indisputable. Turn to any classical music station, and you'll quickly find out how powerful his influence is even today.

Now the question is, if Beethoven could reach within himself and overcome great personal tragedy to influence classical music for centuries to come, what can you do to influence your world?

You don't have to be a great composer, or a great athlete, or a world leader to have influence. Having influence simply means modeling authentic beliefs and behaviors that encourage others to examine who and where they are. Influencers don't have to beat people over the head to get them to buy into their opinion; they simply demonstrate by example. People remember what you do more than what you say.

Mark Chironna, my life coach, says, "Influence is when your reach exceeds your grasp." Ponder that one for a moment. Beethoven released his brilliance, and as a result, nearly two hundred years after his death, we are still feeling his reach.

A person of influence leverages his or her unique gifts, innate talents, and natural abilities to change the world. Each of us is a natural influencer in our own way. Even though you may not think your job, your life, or even your existence on Earth has an impact on anyone, I can assure you that it does. Your life may be the only "bible" that some people will ever read. What example do you set by your words, deeds, and actions?

I invite you to realize there is more brilliance inside you than you've given yourself credit for. You have to decide that your days of tiptoeing through life without making a sound are over. It's time for you to make an impact on your world—your family, friends, job, co-workers, neighbors, and acquaintances.

First, you must change your own world by addressing the eight core areas of your life and polishing your facets. Then you can influence others to change their world. You can't take others on a journey you have not first experienced for yourself; you can only show them where you've been and what you've done.

In my experience, the average person has the ability to significantly influence ten to twenty people in his or her lifetime. And that's exactly what I want you to do! Be a world changer—first change your own world, then help ten to twenty people in your sphere of influence change their worlds. They, in turn, can each help change the worlds of ten to twenty people in their spheres of influence. So although you may directly influence only ten to twenty people, you may *indirectly* influence literally hundreds!

When you know how to open your vault, release your brilliance, and shine brightly, you can lead those still in darkness into the light of possibility. Those who are walking in darkness have forgotten their genius. They don't know how to open the vault and be brilliant. Then they bump into someone who shines brilliantly—like you—and they want to experience brilliance just as you have.

A LIVING DIAMOND:
A Real-Life Story from Tessa

My talent lies in my ability to affect people in such a way that I can make a difference in their lives—be it through empowering them, enhancing their self-esteem and confidence, giving them the courage to make decisions, or simply showing them their strengths, abilities, and positive attributes.

I discovered this talent when I started teaching at the high school level. Even though I was young, just twenty, the feedback from my pupils and their parents allowed me to recognize this gift. Once I moved into the corporate world, ongoing feedback from colleagues, business contacts, clients, and people who attended my training courses reinforced my confidence in my abilities.

I've learned through years of training that there are many, many people who undermine themselves and limit their opportunities because they don't believe in themselves. It gives me immense satisfaction and enjoyment to know that almost every day, I have the opportunity to make a positive impact on someone. It's been a wonderful motivator for me, not only personally, but also professionally. I've come to realize that the gifts of compassion, caring, listening, and selflessness are very precious. Whenever possible, I try to use my gifts to enhance my relationships with people and leave where I can a "touch."

By allowing your light to shine on others, you enlarge their capacity for expectation. And expectation is the breeding ground for brilliance. If you don't expect it, you won't get it. I believe it is your responsibility to not only seek, find, and release your hidden brilliance, but to help others do the same. Lead others to find the light that will illuminate their journey. Without it, they will continue to stumble through life in the darkness. Furthermore, their children—who, like them, were born with genius and full of potential—will likely also live in darkness.

Inspired Brilliance is a term I coined to describe how you can influence your world. To inspire means "to breathe life into" or "the act of influencing and moving the intellect and emotions." Your responsibility here on Earth is to breathe life into every person you meet and influence every situation, circumstance, problem, or opportunity you encounter. You were born to infuse others with your brilliance. Be a vitamin instead of an aspirin to the world around you.

Not too long ago, I was in Johannesburg, South Africa, on a business trip. My host introduced me to the term *ubuntu* (pronounced /ùbúntú/), a traditional African concept that means "I am because you are. You are because I am." The principle of *ubuntu* is humanity toward others . . . the notion that a person "becomes human" through other people. The impact and weight of this word moved me. I realized at the moment I learned it that I am supposed to breathe life into everyone who comes into my space and help them uncover the gifts, talents, skills, and abilities they were born with. My mission is to make the greatest impact on your life for the time you're in my space.

How about you? How will you influence others in your world? When you understand and operate as if you exist for others, your life will never be the same.

PERSONAL APPRAISAL

I invite you to answer the following questions:

1. Whom do you influence personally and professionally? How do you know that you're assisting them in releasing their brilliance?
2. Who are the mentors, coaches, and influencers in your life? How often do you reconnect with them to stay brilliant?
3. What one thing can you do to brilliantly influence the next generation?

DIAMOND POLISHING

Here are three action steps you can take to polish your facets and change your world:

1. List three things you are currently doing to influence the world around you. If you can't think of three, include things you'd like to do that would make a difference. Then think about and write down the action steps you need to take in order to make them happen.

2. Learn to laugh. The kind of laughter I'm talking about comes from a deep place in your soul. It is not a smirk or a grin; it is a bellyaching laugh. When you laugh, you come alive emotionally. All those around you will feel your brilliant, radiating energy. Your light will illuminate their darkness. As you polish yourself, you polish others.

3. Examine the relationships, resources, and situations that influence your life. Do they reveal your brilliance or dim it?

♦ Visit www.ReleasingBrilliance.com for more resources, exercises, tips, and tools for changing your world.

A Gem for You
Release your brilliance . . . be a vitamin instead of an aspirin to the world around you.

CARAT: DECIDE HOW BIG YOU WANT TO BE

"THE TRAGEDY OF LIFE IS OFTEN NOT IN OUR FAILURE, BUT RATHER IN OUR COMPLACENCY; NOT IN OUR DOING TOO MUCH, BUT RATHER IN OUR DOING TOO LITTLE; NOT IN OUR LIVING ABOVE OUR ABILITY, BUT RATHER IN OUR LIVING BELOW OUR CAPACITIES."

—BENJAMIN E. MAYS, SCHOLAR

If you've ever given or received a diamond engagement ring, you probably know something about diamond carats—or at least you know that when it comes to diamonds, the more carats the better. A carat is the measure of a diamond's weight—one carat weighs 0.2 grams. Carat weight does not affect a diamond's quality; it simply measures weight and therefore size. Larger diamonds are more valuable because they are more rare and more sought after than smaller stones of the same quality. A five-carat stone is worth far more than five one-carat stones of the same quality.

The tradition of giving diamond engagement rings began in 1477 when Archduke Maximilian of Austria bought his future wife, Mary of Burgundy, a diamond big enough to blind anyone with its brilliance. This tradition of giving large diamond rings spread throughout the Judeo-Christian world. Since that time, men have often spent two to three times their monthly salaries to purchase the largest-carat diamond they could afford to give their future wives. Let's face it: When it comes to diamonds, bigger really is better.

How does this relate to your quest to unlock the vault and release your diamond brilliance? There is no question that you are going to be a diamond of exceptional clarity, color, and cut. The question is, how big a diamond are you going to be? Just a small glimmer or the brightest dazzler the world has ever seen? Do you see only the limits of your abilities, or do you see unlimited possibilities? You've played small long enough. Stop diminishing your belief in yourself to accommodate someone else's limited thinking and vision. Anyone holding you back doesn't recognize your gifts.

Carats represent the size of your thinking—the possibilities you see for yourself. If you want to expand your brilliance, expand your thinking. If you intend to live a big, brilliant life, you've got to think beyond your current comfort level. You've got to take a quantum leap. You've got to become a *Brillianaire*™.

Guy Laliberté, an accordion player, and Daniel Gauthier, a street circus animator, and their hippie friends from Canada were one park bench away from vagrancy arrest as they toured in a patched-up van to various art and street festivals. Then, in 1987, Laliberté gambled on a make-or-break gig in California at the Los Angeles Festival.

"We went down there barely paying for the gasoline," he recalls. "The festival had no advance money. So I said, 'I'll take the risk, but give me some publicity and the opening-night slot.' It was a hit. The next day, the scalpers were making money from us. But if we had failed, we would have had no money to bring our equipment back to Quebec."

Laliberté wanted to be big, so he thought big. Today, gymnasts, jugglers, dancers, divers, clowns, musicians, and swimmers release their brilliance through Cirque du Soleil's permanent shows in Las Vegas and Orlando and touring shows around the world. This is a true example of taking a leap of faith and seeing the possibilities of unlimited potential.

How big do you see your future?

Today I invite you to grow into the tallest redwood tree—don't be content to simply be a blade of grass. Take a quantum leap and live life beyond your fingers and toes. Be the huge-carat diamond you were meant to be.

A GEM FOR YOU

If you want to expand your brilliance,
expand your thinking.

FACET: CREATE SPIRITUAL WEALTH

"WHEN YOU EXAMINE THE LIVES OF THE MOST INFLUENTIAL PEOPLE WHO HAVE EVER WALKED AMONG US, YOU DISCOVER ONE THREAD THAT WINDS THROUGH THEM ALL. THEY HAVE BEEN ALIGNED FIRST WITH THEIR SPIRITUAL NATURE AND ONLY THEN WITH THEIR PHYSICAL SELVES."

—ALBERT EINSTEIN, PHYSICIST

Do you know people who spend their entire paychecks on consumer items just to impress people they don't like with things they can't afford? We've been hoodwinked into believing that if we wear the most expensive clothes, drive the newest cars, live in the best neighborhoods, eat at the finest restaurants, and attend invitation-only events, then we are "wealthy."

Please understand . . . there is nothing wrong with enjoying the finer things in life. Nor is it wrong to aspire to upgrade your standard of living. However, if your only motive is to impress others, then you may discover that you're cash rich but spiritually poor. The trappings of luxury won't fill your spiritual needs. And all the material possessions in the world won't buy you an answer to the question burning in your heart: "Why am I here?"

When most people think about wealth, they think of financial or material wealth. I think we need to expand that concept. I believe true wealth is a spiritual subject. Wealth is more than a paycheck, a 401(k) plan, a bonus, a stock portfolio, a trust fund, or a retirement plan. Wealth is a belief system, a mindset. Wealthy people never settle; they don't accept the status quo. Wealthy people push the envelope; they want "first class." People with impoverished thinking take what is given to them and never ask for more. Those who are spiritually bankrupt are afraid to become the person they could be. They live beneath their spiritual privilege and constantly settle for what life hands them.

If you intend to be spiritually wealthy, you must adopt a new mindset and mentally relocate to the penthouse in your spirit. There is nothing for you in the basement of life. All the good things are at the top. Don't settle for the bottom floor when you could be living in the luxurious top-floor penthouse.

When negative things happen to you, don't become discouraged. Encourage yourself by speaking and believing a simple truth—that this, too, shall pass. Don't allow setbacks to become a permanent way of life and quell your spirit. Break out of the box of limiting beliefs that has you trapped. How you see yourself determines what you will attract to your life. Believe in yourself and the power of your abilities. Expect good things to happen and know that you are worthy of them. Remember, you are rich. You are valuable. You are priceless!

This is not hype, nor is it some New Age psychobabble. This is a timeless truth about the unlimited potential hidden inside you. Your spiritual wealth will grow exponentially when you invest time in building your self-worth instead of your net worth.

The Good Book says to love your neighbor as you love yourself. And although that saying might seem obvious and trite, truly loving and appreciating the person you are probably doesn't come easily. If someone were to examine how you talk to yourself and treat yourself, would they see a kind and loving person? I think you'd be shocked to discover how harmful some people can be to themselves. If they treated others the way they treat themselves, they might very well end up in jail.

You will never be a huge-carat diamond until you can love yourself and accept yourself unconditionally. You can't constantly beat yourself up and expect to release your brilliance in a profound, world-changing way. No matter how much you polish your other facets and do all the right things on the outside, if you haven't learned to love yourself, you won't be as big or as brilliant as God intended you to be. Focus on building your self-worth and accumulating spiritual wealth, and you will reap wondrous rewards in the future.

In ancient times, diamonds were prized for their spiritual connection. The ancient Romans believed diamonds were splinters from falling stars; the Greeks, that they were tears of the gods. Plato even wrote about diamonds as living beings, embodying celestial spirits.

We must think of ourselves in that same spiritual way. The great thinkers of our time say that we are not human beings having a spiritual experience, but spiritual beings having a human experience here on Earth. Our diamond brilliance is spiritually based. If this is true, everything you need to succeed comes from your spirit.

Your purpose, then, is to grow your spiritual wealth to the point where you can share it and give it away. Use your skills, abilities, gifts, time, and energy to fulfill your Universal Assignment and serve others. By investing your life's energy in meaningful and purposeful activities, you increase your spiritual wealth and find happiness and internal bliss. You will accumulate spiritual wealth once you learn how to live from the inside out, instead of the outside in.

I believe spiritual wealth has nothing to do with the acquisition of material possessions. For me, it has everything to do with finding complete internal wholeness, whereby I accept all that God has given me and leverage it to brilliantly shine every day of my existence. I didn't hang the sun or the moon. I am unable to count the stars in the night sky. I can't even see the air that I breathe. But in my spirit, I know that all of these things have been provided for my enjoyment and my use.

My spiritual wealth does not increase or decrease with the fluctuations of the stock market or the amount of money in my pocket. I am wealthy because I have embraced who I am and because I like who I am becoming. If you don't accept me for who I am, it's okay. I'll still sleep well at night. And I'll still love you for who you are—a spiritual being, just like me, in search of a treasure called spiritual wealth.

PERSONAL APPRAISAL
I invite you to answer the following questions:

1. Are you cash rich but spiritually bankrupt? If yes, why? What can you do to change the situation?
2. When was the last time you shared a kind word with someone that lifted that person's spirits?
3. What spiritual wealth inheritance will you leave for the next generation?

A LIVING DIAMOND:
A Real-Life Story from Gretchen

I used to believe that I could work and will my way to brilliance and success . . . I discovered that it takes more than that.

I've always focused on educating myself in one form or another while creating and working in business. And I've always been the kind of person who is motivated and inspired by seeking and finding the truth in all things, not only to provide greater depth, meaning, and understanding about life, but also to be better equipped to face life's challenges.

My quest for truth occurred in the detached, self-interested manner that our society breeds so readily. Beneath this drive for the truth was a need for acceptance, recognition, and a secure personal position. Like many others, I had an ego to feed, and I found myself in the conventional battle to "get ahead," sometimes without having full comprehension of or taking responsibility for the consequences.

And yet every experience I've had along the way was there for a specific purpose—to teach me something I needed to know, regardless of whether I was physically or emotionally ready for it. Little did I know that I was putting in place the building blocks that would one day allow me to realize what some refer to as my "brilliance."

Then I had a life experience that I was completely unprepared for—the death of a special loved one. I went into deep mourning and shock. I was at a loss as to how to cope with my future. Over time, I recognized that the spirit of my loved one surely couldn't have vanished. He was too valuable, too special! He represented purity and love . . . how could this end?

Somehow, this experience became a catalyst for change. All the study, all the hard work, all the truth-seeking began to pay off in new and unexpected ways. I finally knew that the infinite domain existed and that we are all "one," rather than—as in the conventional view—individuals sharing this planet. All the quantum physics clicked into place. I realized that the world of individuals—which I used to think resembled the bar scene in *Star Wars*, with more differences than similarities—was an illusion. We are connected by a common spiritual force, a conscious shared intelligence, and its driving force is love.

With this truth, my motivations in life shifted dramatically from the self-centered, ego-conscious drive for perfection and getting ahead to a deep desire to serve all of mankind. Call it brilliance or call it finding one's purpose . . . the truth is the same.

DIAMOND POLISHING

Here are three action steps you can take to polish your facets and create spiritual wealth.

1. List three things you can do to increase your self-worth instead of your net worth.
2. Write down all of the wonderful blessings in your life and marvel at how truly wealthy you are.
3. Identify ten positive things that happened to you this week and share them with your Brilliandeer. Then ask him or her to share the same with you.

A GEM FOR YOU

Releasing your brilliance is about increasing your self-worth, not your net worth.

FACET: CRYSTALLIZE YOUR MOMENTS OF TRUTH

"TO EVERY PERSON THERE COMES THAT SPECIAL MOMENT WHEN HE IS TAPPED ON THE SHOULDER TO DO A VERY SPECIAL THING UNIQUE TO HIM. WHAT A TRAGEDY IF THAT MOMENT FINDS HIM UNPREPARED FOR THE WORK THAT WOULD BE HIS FINEST HOUR."

—WINSTON CHURCHILL, BRITISH PRIME MINISTER

In 1903, the Wright brothers made history in Kitty Hawk, North Carolina, with the first successful airplane flight. With Orville at the controls, the plane flew 120 feet (37 meters) and was in the air twelve seconds. The brothers made three more flights that day. The longest, by Wilbur, was 852 feet (260 meters) in fifty-nine seconds. Just imagine what was going through their minds as they attempted to fly a machine. Every flight that day was a "moment of truth" that created positive momentum to try again. Each effort increased their faith, courage, tenacity, and strength.

The *Merriam-Webster Collegiate Dictionary* defines *moment of truth* as "a crucial moment, a critical or decisive time on which much depends." Moments of truth are those profound times in our lives when critical pieces of our life's puzzle are revealed to us. These "aha!" moments stop you in your tracks and take your breath away. It's as if a light switches on in your mind, something clicks, and suddenly you have more clarity about the meaning and purpose of your life.

Some moments of truth are magical, joyful occasions when you have the opportunity to celebrate the synchronicity of life. Others occur when you arrive at a crossroad in your life and must decide which direction to go. And finally, some moments of truth are major turning points—times when tragedy or trauma sensitizes you to the big picture, the larger purpose of your life.

Every moment of truth has the power and the potential to shape you and shape your future. Each one can be a catalyst for change—if you let it. But first you must pay attention to those moments and invest your energy in crystallizing their meaning.

The word *crystallize* has at least two definitions: "to make clear" and "to give a permanent form to." Interestingly, both of these definitions fit our use here. When you crystallize your moments of truth, you will see your life more clearly, and then you can use that insight to make permanent, lasting change.

How do you crystallize a moment of truth? The process involves three steps.

1. **Be present in the moment.** Take everything in. Focus on the moment at hand using all your senses. Simply

observe the situation without any preconceived notions about what it all means.

2. **Discover the meaning of the moment.** Every moment of truth has a purpose. Seek the truth of the life lesson by asking the questions "How does this experience relate to my life? What am I to learn from this?" Be open and allow the moment to teach you.

3. **Apply the lesson to your life.** Now that you know the truth or have the missing piece of the puzzle, what should you do to create permanent, lasting change? What can you do to crystallize the lesson in your life?

You can create forward momentum in your life by seizing your "aha!" moments. Your life is a continuous string of moments, and each moment presents a lesson. If you use each lesson to change some aspect of your life, you will create tremendous momentum. Momentum, in turn, creates monumental results. If you don't like the results you're getting, examine the moments that comprise your life. Use your momentum to open the vault and release the brilliance that has been hiding there for so many years. Then, use your momentum again to take a quantum leap and live a big-carat life.

I believe if Orville and Wilbur Wright were alive today, they would tell you that each moment contains the seeds of unlimited possibility, the opportunities to create life-changing momentum.

- Every optimistic thought about the future creates momentum.
- Every positive word you say contains creative potential that creates momentum.
- Every fear you face and overcome creates momentum.
- Every opportunity you take advantage of creates momentum.
- Every setback is an invitation to regain your focus and create momentum.

Today I invite you to maximize and crystallize your personal moments of truth. When you learn to leverage the lessons of these moments, you can change your life and shape your future. Moments of truth are not to be avoided; they are to be seized and used to create positive, life-changing momentum.

PERSONAL APPRAISAL

I invite you to answer the following questions:

1. When was the last time you experienced a moment of truth? Were you aware of the meaning of the moment? What did you do about it afterward?
2. What can you do to master the moments of your life and leverage their value?
3. How can you learn to be more "present in the moment"?

A LIVING DIAMOND:
A Real-Life Story from Mercedes

When you're twenty-one, you have your entire life ahead of you. At least that's what I thought on the morning of my twenty-first birthday. But by day's end, my parents and 158 other people were dead, and I was critically injured, stranded in the mountains of Colombia. Up until then, I'd had a near picture-perfect life: a great family, a successful college career, many close friends, and a wonderful new boyfriend. But all that came to an end on December 20, 1995, due to a "series of human errors."

I am one of only four people who lived through what experts have called an "unsurvivable" airplane crash. During the eighteen hours I waited to be rescued—and again at the hospital when doctors gave me only a 20 to 30 percent chance of survival—I thought my life was likely over. I prayed for a second chance at life and vowed that if given that gift, I would make it count.

My life changed forever that day. The crash was a turning point in my life and the first of many critical moments of truth. It served as a wake-up call—an unforgettable reminder that I should endeavor every single day to achieve my personal best and to live a life full of gratitude. And it was a foreshadowing of things to come, of challenges I could never have imagined. There were many more physical and emotional battles ahead: waking up alone in a hospital in a foreign country, hearing of my parents' death from reporters on live TV, enduring five surgeries, learning to walk again, traveling by airplane just one month after being released from the hospital, calling my parents' answering machine just to hear their voices, and overcoming permanent physical limitations. The hardest one of all was accepting and dealing with the loss of my parents at such an early age.

By the grace of God, I was granted another chance at life. I suppose I could have played the victim card and been bitter about my fate. Instead, I chose to live . . . to *truly* live. Through the darkness of those months after the crash, the choices I intentionally made at each moment of truth became a blueprint for my life. To this day, those same choices continue to give me the fuel and the momentum I need in my daily quest to live a fulfilling, successful life.

When it became evident that I would live, I committed to myself, to God, and to my parents and the 158 other people who died that day to make my second chance count. So several years later, I left a lucrative job in medical sales and became a motivational speaker to spread the message that there are no automatic tomorrows. Too many people operate under the assumption that there will always be an automatic tomorrow in which they'll have the luxury of fixing today's problems, righting today's wrongs, and doing the things they wished they'd done today. As a result, they have no urgency in their lives. They allow themselves to be crippled by their circumstances and become stuck in the rut of survival mode, unable to enjoy all that life has to offer.

Tragedy is a powerful teacher. It has taught me that

our destiny is determined not by what happens to us, but by the choices we make. Every morning that we wake up, we are given the gift of a second chance at life. With every new day, we have the opportunity to get back on track, to find peace and happiness, and to be the person each of us was meant to be. *What are you going to do with your second chance today?*

DIAMOND POLISHING

Here are three action steps you can take to polish your facets and crystallize your moments of truth.

1. Identify the three moments of truth that have had the greatest impact on your life. How did they permanently change you?
2. Commit to capturing your moments of truth in a journal. Be sure to include the meaning of each moment and how you intend to crystallize that meaning.
3. Write down three things you can do to create forward momentum in your life.

A Gem for You

Moments of truth create momentum,
and momentum leads to monumental results.

FACET: EXPAND YOUR POSSIBILITIES

**"THE WRIGHT BROTHERS FLEW THROUGH THE SMOKE
SCREEN OF IMPOSSIBILITY."**

–DOROTHEA BRANDE, WRITER

According to a recent study, there are seven million millionaires in the United States. With a population of almost 300 million people, why only seven million? Why aren't there more millionaires? What's wrong with the rest of us?

Absolutely nothing! The problem is that we think small and we play small. We think it's impossible to achieve our hearts' desires, so we never hope for anything bigger than the space we're standing in at the moment. We might dream big, but we're afraid to realize that dream and become who we've always wanted to be. Certainly there are brilliant people who do great things, but most of us don't see that possibility for ourselves.

We live in a society that encourages mediocrity and conformity. Most of us are taught to go to school, get an education, get a good job, get married, buy a house, and . . . settle down. We've been conditioned to *conform* and *settle*, to accept mediocrity and not to rock the boat. We've been trained to believe the lie that says, "This is what life has dealt me, and this is what I must accept."

People who play small attract into their space everything that appears to be impossible. People who believe bigger and better things are possible attract bigger and better opportunities, situations, and circumstances. These big-carat people make the impossible possible. People who refuse to settle for less and who push beyond the limits are the ones who are brilliantly successful. Thinking small, speaking small, and acting small is not in their DNA. Even when their backs are against the wall, they hear a voice speaking to their spirit, urging, "All things are possible if you believe."

Now, does believing in possibility mean desiring a mansion on a hill, a Rolls-Royce in the garage, and servants at your beck and call? The answer is no. Big-carat people are not controlled by material things or worldly wealth, although those things are certainly nice and often come with the territory.

Believing in possibility means choosing to be a destinorian, not a historian. A destinorian studies the path of destiny. Destinorians are tuned in to the universal frequency of the "next big thing." They prepare themselves to create the future rather than be controlled by it. They're open to their feelings as well as their thoughts. As my life coach, Dr. Mark Chironna, once said to me: "Thinking happens in the mind; but you feel your way into the future by listening to your spirit, which is located in the vault of your heart."

Wherever you are right now in life—employed or unemployed, happy or bored, with big dreams or no dreams—decide now to view everything in your life as a brilliant opportunity. However you feel about your situation, I truly believe that if the impossible became possible for me, it's possible for you, too. Releasing your brilliance is about looking for and leveraging the countless options and unlimited possibilities that exist for you.

Maybe you don't want people to make a big deal over you. Maybe you'd rather play small and have everyone think you're modest, grounded, and humble. Well, for those who want to think small, go ahead. This message is for those of you who have played small long enough and are ready to release your brilliance in a grand, king-sized way.

Everything is possible when you accept that impossibility is not an option. Become a possibility thinker. Possibility thinking is believing ALL things are possible—not just some things, not just the easy things—ALL things.

It is true there are some things in life you can't control, and I suppose you could categorize those as impossible. However, I believe even the things you can't control are possible. Why? Consider this insight from W. N. Murray in his book *The Scottish Himalayan Expedition*: "The moment one definitely commits oneself,

A LIVING DIAMOND:
A Real-Life Story from Terry

We all believed anything was possible when we were kids. I think everyone has that gift as a child. Fortunately, I never completely lost that ability. It's been shaken, but somehow my faith in greater possibilities remains.

When I was very young, I went through a stint in which I wanted to become a doctor. My parents had a set of medical encyclopedias that just sat on the bookshelf collecting dust. Well, I figured if I wanted to be a doctor, all I had to do was learn what doctors know. Every day, I would come home, dust off one of those books, and just read. In my heart, I thought if I read enough and knew enough, then in time I would be a doctor.

Today, I still apply that same approach to life . . . nothing is impossible if you're equipped with enough knowledge, faith, and confidence to tackle it. I believe that with the right amount of preparation, people will ultimately go where their hearts lead them.

Now, when friends talk about things they want to do, I get on the Internet and start researching information for them. I want to do all I can to help them make their dreams real. One friend told me she wanted to learn Spanish and travel, but I never saw her taking steps to pursue that goal. For her birthday, I gave her a book about Puerto Rico—*en Español!* Concrete actions render concrete results. If she wants to accomplish something, then I also want that for her. And as a friend, I'm willing to take action to support her.

Unfortunately, as I've grown older, I've realized that many times we're more willing to act on and support our friends' and families' dreams than our own. We get into a comfortable groove and instead of disrupting that comfort to fulfill our desires, we simply accept the status quo and move on through life. Essentially, we'd rather watch from the comfort of the stands than get out there on the playing field.

I never became a doctor. But by taking action toward that goal, I learned enough about medicine to know it simply wasn't for me. That freed me to follow other dreams in my life. I have no regrets about not pursuing that path. But what if the expense of attending medical school and the years of interning required had prevented me from ever even exploring it? Maybe I'd still be wishing for my own practice, and I would have wasted my life lamenting a dream that was never really meant for me.

There are always opportunities for those who see the possibilities!

then Providence moves too. All sorts of things occur to help one that would otherwise never have occurred. A whole stream of events issues from the decision, raising in one's favor all manner of unforeseen incidents and meetings and material assistance, which no man could have dreamed would have come his way."

Yes, I truly believe ALL things are possible. How about you?

Engage in possibility thinking by making a decision to be bigger. It's that simple. It all comes down to one decision—a decision to believe. Because the issue isn't that some things are impossible. The issue is that you *think* and you *believe* some things are impossible. Once you change your thinking and commit to the belief that ALL things *are* possible, Heaven and Earth will move to make it so. I am here to tell you from experience that if you will just make a decision and then put one foot in front of the other, you can, in fact, achieve whatever your heart desires. You have the potential to become so much more than what you are. No one can stop you but you.

Is it possible that there exists a diamond so flawless and so big that the world's diamond experts consider it priceless?

It's not only possible, it's true.

The De Beers Millennium Star was discovered in the Republic of the Congo in the early 1990s. It took more than three years for diamond cutters to shape the stone with lasers. What emerged was the world's only internally and externally flawless, 203-carat, pear-shaped diamond. It was unveiled as the centerpiece of the De Beers Millennium diamond collection. De Beers created the collection as a way to symbolize the world's hopes and dreams for the future.

Is it possible that *you* could be a diamond so great in size that the hope, light, and brilliance you bring to the world is priceless?

It's not only possible, it's true.

PERSONAL APPRAISAL

I invite you to answer the following questions:

1. Are you exploring and living a life of possibility, or are you playing small?
2. Have you settled for something less than what you desire because you think what you desire is impossible? Has settling become a permanent way of life? Examine the situation. Is it really impossible, or do you only think it's impossible?
3. How big can you see yourself, your reach, and your influence?

DIAMOND POLISHING

Here are three action steps you can take to polish your facets and expand your possibilities.

1. Write down the names of three people who have overcome extraordinary obstacles and find out how they made the "impossible" possible.
2. Find a life coach or mentor who will challenge you to get rid of CZ thinking and practice possibility thinking.
3. Every day, schedule some reflection time to quiet your soul, away from the hustle and bustle of the day, and write in your journal. A journal is a portfolio of possibilities, a place to capture your thoughts and dreams for what could be possible in your life. Journaling aids you in processing what is in your soul and organizing it into coherent thoughts. That's important because the quality of your life is determined by the quality of your thoughts.

♦ Visit www.ReleasingBrilliance.com for more resources,
  exercises, tips, and tools for identifying and eliminating
  your Brilliance Blockers™ and expanding your
  possibilities.

A Gem for You
*Everything is possible when you accept that
impossibility is not an option.*

EUREKA! I *AM* A BRILLIANT DIAMOND!

"THE CALL TO ADVENTURE COMES IN MANY WAYS,
BOTH SUBTLE AND EXPLICIT, OVER THE YEARS. IT IS
A CALL TO SERVICE, GIVING OUR LIVES OVER TO
SOMETHING LARGER THAN OURSELVES, THE CALL TO
BECOME WHAT WE WERE MEANT TO BECOME–THE CALL
TO ACHIEVE OUR VITAL DESIGN."

–JOSEPH JAWORSKI, AUTHOR

Allow me to project onto the movie screen of your mind an image of your future—an image of you releasing your diamond brilliance and fulfilling your destiny. Take a few moments to think about what that would be like.

Now, imagine the scene using all of your senses. What do you see? Paint the picture as vividly as you can with all the colors of a painter's palette. Do you see yourself being greeted by enthusiastic, engaged co-workers and leaders as you start an exciting new job? Or perhaps you see freshly printed business cards that represent the culmination of years of hard work and commitment.

What do you hear? Is it the sound of hundreds of people applauding your accomplishments, or the muffled, sleepy voice of a child snuggled into the crook of your neck? What does your brilliance taste like? Like the finest Champagne with which you toast your success? Or the exotic spice of new and different foods sampled in restaurants and cafés around the world?

What do you smell? Yes, you can smell your brilliance! Perhaps it's the scent of perfume or cologne as you dress in fine clothing in preparation for a meeting with a key person of influence. Or the smell of fresh paint and new carpet as you open the doors of your business for the first time or step into your brand-new home.

The touch of brilliance may feel like the musical instrument on which you display your artistic genius, the weight of your first published book, or the comfort of another's embrace.

Now, imagine what it feels like on the inside when you find the combination to the vault, unlock it, and release your diamond brilliance. Isn't it liberating to no longer have to compare yourself to everyone else? What do you experience when you rediscover your incredible value and worth after all these years? How does it feel to be authentically *You* and to find your voice, your light?

In the last year, I've asked more than one thousand people the following question: "How does it feel when you're releasing your brilliance, when your soul and your spirit are fully engaged in an activity that makes you come alive?" Here are just a few of the most common answers.

- Complete
- Totally focused
- Effortless
- In the flow
- Connected
- Fulfilled
- Confident
- Absolutely resilient

For me, releasing my diamond brilliance creates a sense of exhilaration, *a deep sense of enjoyment that has become the benchmark for what my life should feel like every day.* I call it Engaged Brilliance—the melding and synergizing of all the parts of your internal and external being. It's what you get when you combine the clarity of profound insight with pure white belief and diamond-polishing action. Engaged Brilliance is the final "click" of the lock on the vault where your diamond potential resides.

Many people believe in a sixth sense. They call it different things: perception, intuition, mindsight, even ESP. I, too, believe there is a sixth sense, but I believe it is a sense of faith. Go back to the picture of your future in your mind, and use that sense now. . . .

Is it really so hard to believe that it's you in the picture? Don't you see that the person in the picture is who you were meant to be? In truth, it's who you are already; that person is simply buried within you. Your brilliance is your essence, an extension of you. Deep in your soul, do you believe that you're a brilliant diamond? Do you have the faith that you can polish your edges and reveal the diamond within you? Give up the person you've been and choose to become the brilliant diamond God intended you to be. What are you waiting for?

No matter what has happened to you in life—bad luck, bad circumstances, or bad choices—decide *now* to pick yourself up and be brilliant. I'm inviting you to transition from simply existing to living passionately, to transform from dull to dazzling. All the tools you need to release your brilliance are within you. They've been there all along, since you were a gleam in your father's eye and a speck in your mother's womb. These tools are your thoughts, your beliefs, and your actions. They are the combination to the vault.

You may recall that at the beginning of this book, I suggested you read it once all the way through—and here you are. Now it's time to get to work. If all you do is read this book, more than likely, nothing in your life will change. Until you find an Accountability Partner, your own Brilliandeer, and complete the Personal Appraisal and Diamond Polishing exercises, there will be no Evolutionary Transformation for you. To open the vault and release your brilliance, you have to DO something.

Earlier in the book, you identified your then current position on the Brilliance Continuum. Now, I invite you to complete that same exercise again, indicating where you are on the continuum *today.*

EXERCISE: *The Brilliance Continuum*

Below is a model to help you identify your current ability to release your brilliance. Dazzling, of course, is what you're striving for. Draw a vertical line to indicate where you believe are right now on the Brilliance Continuum.

DULL   DAZZLING

Compare your position today on the continuum with your position when you started your transformation. There . . . do you see the change? You've already polished your facets enough that you've moved forward on the continuum. As you continue to polish and perfect the fifteen facets, you'll discover more areas that need attention. Releasing your brilliance is a journey, not a destination. It's a continuous process of polishing and reshaping the diamond that is you, of becoming more dazzling with each passing day.

When you engage your spiritual, mental, and physical energy in pursuing something you believe in, the vault containing your diamond brilliance is opened from the inside out. The word *diamond* comes from the Greek word *adamas*, which means "unconquerable." When you're living your diamond brilliance, there's no limit to what you can achieve, become, or do.

Living your brilliance isn't about achieving material

wealth or prestige, although those things may joyfully come with it. When you release your brilliance, you don't work a job, you fulfill a purpose—you make a difference. Design your life around your Universal Assignment and then come alive to the reality that you *are* destined for greatness.

A diamond's brilliance is measured by something called Return of Light—the amount of light returned through the top of the diamond and directed at the beholder. Your diamond brilliance can also be measured by Return of Light—how much light you release and shine on the world.

In 1866, a shepherd boy named Erasmus Jacobs found a small, shiny stone on the south bank of the Orange River near Hopetown, South Africa. The stone eventually found its way to a doctor, one of the few people in the area who knew anything about minerals and gems. The doctor identified it as a 21.25-carat diamond. It was named the Eureka Diamond, and it started a diamond-prospecting rush similar to the California Gold Rush.

Eureka literally means "I have found it" in Greek. The expression is attributed to the Greek mathematician Archimedes, who was so excited by his discovery of how to determine the purity of gold in the third century BC that he jumped out of his bath and ran home naked, all the while shouting, "Eureka! Eureka!"

In current times, we still use the word to express triumph when we find or discover something of importance or value. And is there anything more important or valuable than discovering your diamond brilliance?

I've been on a journey for the last twenty years to find my own brilliance and to figure out how to let it shine. I realize now that I'm here to help others find the combination to their hidden vaults, open them, reveal their brilliance, and light up the world. It is my sincere hope and prayer that I have, in some small way, helped you discover the amazing brilliance that I am certain lies within you. I have faith in you. You have what it takes to polish your facets and transform yourself into an enormous, dazzling diamond.

When that time comes—when you find your brilliance—I invite you to contact me. (My contact information is at the back of the book.) E-mail me, call me, or introduce yourself to me in person and say just one word: *"Eureka!"*

Then I will know you have found and released the brilliant diamond that is **You!**

A GEM FOR YOU

*When you engage your spiritual, mental,
and physical energy in something you believe in,
the vault containing your diamond brilliance
is opened from the inside out.*

"WHEN YOU ENGAGE IN WORK THAT TAPS YOUR TALENT
AND FUELS YOUR PASSION—THAT RISES OUT OF A GREAT
NEED IN THE WORLD THAT YOU FEEL DRAWN BY
CONSCIENCE TO MEET—THEREIN LIES YOUR VOICE,
YOUR CALLING, YOUR SOUL'S CODE."

—DR. STEPHEN COVEY, AUTHOR

GEMS FOR YOU

- Your geography and your biography do not determine your destiny.
- It takes a diamond to cut a diamond.
- Everything you need to be brilliant is already inside you.
- Your Universal Assignment is not to touch everyone; it is to touch *someone*.
- You release your diamond brilliance when you operate in your natural intelligence.
- Diamond people understand the connection between thoughts, beliefs, actions, and outcomes.
- Your goal is to discover "nature's fingerprints" on your life.
- When your motives are authentic, you attract what's in your highest good.
- Once a year, evaluate the eight Crown Facets of your life.

- Every choice point is an opportunity to realign yourself with your inner truth.
- Faith is your belief in tomorrow when today is nothing short of chaos.
- Intuition is peace that surpasses all understanding.
- Are you an authentic diamond, or are you a CZ?
- Action makes you stronger.
- Are you friend rich but relationship poor?
- We are afraid of the sheer power of our brilliance, of being the dazzling diamonds we were meant to be.
- You are the prophet of your future. Use Life Language to create your brilliant future.
- High-impact habits accelerate the process of opening the vault and releasing your brilliance.
- Release your brilliance . . . be a vitamin instead of an aspirin to the world around you.
- If you want to expand your brilliance, expand your thinking.
- Releasing your brilliance is about increasing your self-worth, not your net worth.
- Moments of truth create momentum, and momentum leads to monumental results.
- Everything is possible when you accept that impossibility is not an option.
- When you engage your spiritual, mental, and physical energy in something you believe in, the vault containing your diamond brilliance is opened from the inside out.

ACKNOWLEDGMENTS

I want to thank my brilliant wife and partner in all things, Renee, for having patience with me as I gave birth to this book. Thanks to my brilliant children, Daniel and Madison—you are my most valuable diamonds. I am blessed to be your father.

Dale Cochran, I appreciate you opening a major door for me. I will be forever grateful. Joe DiDomizio and Sara Hinckley of Hudson Group, thank you for taking a risk and introducing me to HarperCollins. Thanks to Keith Harrell for being the catalyst and the connector in helping me release my brilliance.

Jan Miller, Shannon Marven, and Cheri Gillis, my literary team at Dupree/Miller, thanks for your wisdom and guidance during this publishing endeavor. Joe Tessitore, Ethan Friedman, George Bick, Angie Lee, Sarah Brown, and all of the incredible diamonds at Harper-Collins who made this project possible, thank you so much. From today into eternity, I will call you "Oh Brilliant Ones."

Special thanks to Diane Sears for helping me to uncover the diamonds. Melissa Monogue, thank you for your incredible patience and graphic-design genius. Juli Baldwin, you are my Brilliandeer. Thanks for shaping and polishing me during this tedious book project. You never gave up on me. In your own way, you smiled and kept pulling out the hidden gems and refused to settle for CZ stones. Thank you. Simon believes . . . you are brilliant!

Thank you to my brilliant team at The Belief Institute: Melissa Spencer, Michele Lucia, Lisa Long, and Caroline Bartholomew.

Finally, thank you to my master teacher and life coach, Dr. Mark Chironna, and to all of the other profound influencers in my life: T. D. Jakes, Joseph Garlington, Doug Holladay, Eddie Long, Tudor Bismark, Myles Monroe, Ralph Veerman, Mike Nelson, Mark Victor Hansen, Ken Blanchard, Nido Qubein, and Thom Winninger.

ABOUT THE AUTHOR

Simply put, Simon T. Bailey is a **Catalyst for Brilliance** who invites people to shift their thinking, move off the dime, and change their world from the inside out. A true "category of one," he has an uncommon talent for inspiring people to be accountable to themselves and to continue the change process long after the presentation is over or the book is finished.

Simon is the founder and Chief Belief Officer of The Brilliance Institute, an organization dedicated to building the world's most valuable resource—people. A fresh voice in the business world, he guides organizations and their leaders to the realization that people release their brilliance in environments where they are celebrated rather than tolerated. His counsel helps organizations drive productivity and increase employee retention, which ultimately lead to a brilliant bottom line.

Simon's expertise in leadership, sales, and customer service was honed over two decades with Hyatt Hotels, Walt Disney World Resort,® and the Disney Institute. His clients encompass executives, Fortune 500 companies, and national associations in the United States and abroad.

Simon is the author of four books, including *Simon Says Dream: Live a Passionate Life* and *Simon Believes . . . Brilliant Service* **Is** *the Bottom Line*. In addition to bachelor's and master's degrees, he holds an honorary Doctorate of Divinity degree from Faith Christian University for his global impact.

RELEASE *YOUR* BRILLIANCE

Visit www.releasingbrilliance.com for everything you need to further help you release your brilliance, including a free e-zine, resources, exercises, tips and tools, Simon's Brilliance Blog, the Brillianaire Community, Tele-seminars, Videos, and coaching.

RELEASE THE HIDDEN BRILLIANCE WITHIN YOUR ORGANIZATION

Find out what Verizon, Microsoft, State Farm, The Hudson Group, Embarq, McDonald's Gartner Group, Wellpoint, Metavante, Blue Cross Blue Shield, Wells Fargo, Kaiser Permanente, Walt Disney Swan & Dolphin Resort, National Black MBA, and the Society of Human Resources Management already know: a session with Simon T. Bailey is truly a transformational experience! To learn more, visit www.simontbailey.com or e-mail info@simontbailey.com.

SPECIAL OFFER— *4 STEPS TO RELEASING YOUR BRILLIANCE* DVD

Take the principles presented in the *Release Your Brilliance* book to the next level and transform your life. This special-offer DVD contains new material not included in the book. To receive the *4 Steps to Releasing Your Brilliance* DVD for only $6.95 shipping and handling*, go to www.simontbailey.com or www.releasing brilliance.com.

* You pay nothing except $6.95 Shipping & Handling when delivered inside the continental USA. Please allow 6-8 weeks for delivery. Outside continental USA, Shipping & Handling will be calculated at the time of request. This offer is open to anyone who registers at the above mentioned websites. The offer is effective January 1, 2008 and is valid until December 1, 2009 or while supplies last. This special offer is limited to one per customer; if you would like to purchase additional copies, contact us at info@simontbailey.com. All rights are reserved. This DVD may not be used for any purpose other than the personal viewing of the recipient without the express written permission of Simon T. Bailey and Brilliance Institute, Inc. Duplication or reselling of this DVD is strictly prohibited. This offer will be fulfilled solely by Simon T. Bailey. HarperCollins is not the supplier of this DVD and assumes no liability for any actions on the part of Simon T. Bailey in connection with this offer or the DVD.